Studying Law on the Internet

How to use the internet for learning and study, exams and career development

South Essex College
Further & Higher Education, Thurrock Campus
Woodview Grays Essex RM16 2YR
Tel: 01375 391199 Fax: 01375 373356
Minicom: 01375 362740

Internet Handbooks

Other titles in preparation

Studying
Law
on the internet

How to use the internet for learning and study, exams
and career development

Stephen Hardy

www.internet-handbooks.co.uk

Other titles by the same author

The English Legal System (Studymates)
Law & Lawyers on the Internet (Internet Handbooks)

Dedication – To Dominic, born of the internet age.

344 · 1007 HAR (904)

© Copyright 2001 by Stephen Hardy

First published in 2001 by Internet Handbooks Ltd, Plymbridge House, Estover Road, Plymouth PL6 7PY, United Kingdom.

Customer services tel:	(01752) 202301
Orders fax:	(01752) 202333
Customer services email:	cservs@plymbridge.com
Distributors web site:	http://www.plymbridge.com
Internet Handbooks web site:	http://www.internet-handbooks.co.uk

Note: The contents of this book are offered for the purposes of general guidance only and no liability can be accepted for any loss or expense incurred as a result of relying in particular circumstances on statements made in this book. Readers are advised to check the current position with the appropriate authorities before entering into personal arrangements.

Typeset by PDQ Typesetting, Newcastle-under-Lyme, Staffordshire
Printed and bound by The Cromwell Press Ltd, Trowbridge, Wiltshire.

Contents

Contents . . . .

List of illustrations

Illustrations..

The information revolution has not only changed the lives of individuals, but of industry, commerce and education. As law and technology draw closer together in both learning and practice, the internet has become a rich legal resource for students.

This handbook joins a well-established series in Internet handbooks, but stands apart in that it is the first directly written for law students in order to assist them in finding law easily. The handbook aims to provide a means of learning new skills and guidance on how to monopolise the flexibility and freedom offered by technological developments in law. Above all it aims to meet the needs of students who are seeking advice on how to find the major relevant law web sites, legal information systems, on-line service and Internet legal communities. It is hoped that this handbook will be an essential techno-friendly course companion for every student of law.

Please note that neither the author nor the publisher is responsible for content or opinions expressed on the sites listed, which are primarily intended to offer starting points for students. Also, please remember that the internet is a fast-evolving environment; the appearance of individual pages may change, and links may come and go. If you have some favourite sites you would like to see mentioned in future editions of this book, please email me at the address shown below.

As for the idea upon which this handbook is based, I cannot alone claim the credit, since over the last three years so many of my students have mentioned the need for such a guide and my very foresighted publisher had already observed the market need. Consequently, I thank my students (both past and present), colleagues, my patient publisher (Roger Ferneyhough), various lawyers and others for their assistance and motivation.

All of the web sites shown in this book remain the copyright of their respective owners. The screen shots of web sites were correct at the time of going to press and may appear differently at different times. All trademarks and registered trademarks mentioned in this book are the property of their respective owners.

As ever I thank my wife for her love and support, and accept that any errors or omissions are my own.

If you would like to suggest additional sites for inclusion in a future edition of this book, please send details to the email address below. Happy surfing, and may your legal studies on the net be fruitful.

Stephen Hardy

Manchester School of Management

shardy@internet-handbooks.co.uk

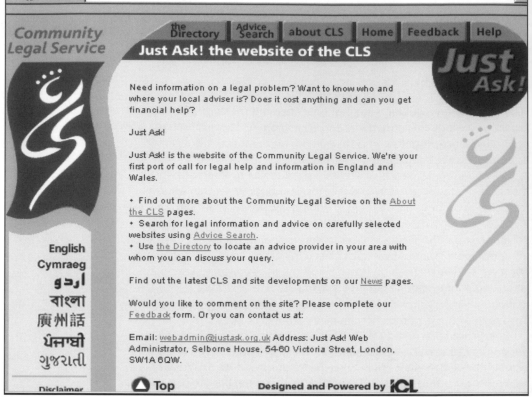

Location: http://www.justask.org.uk/

Community Legal Service

the Directory | Advice Search | about CLS | Home | Feedback | Help

Just Ask! the website of the CLS

Just Ask!

Need information on a legal problem? Want to know who and where your local adviser is? Does it cost anything and can you get financial help?

Just Ask!

Just Ask! is the website of the Community Legal Service. We're your first port of call for legal help and information in England and Wales.

+ Find out more about the Community Legal Service on the About the CLS pages.
+ Search for legal information and advice on carefully selected websites using Advice Search.
+ Use the Directory to locate an advice provider in your area with whom you can discuss your query.

Find out the latest CLS and site developments on our News pages.

Would you like to comment on the site? Please complete our Feedback form. Or you can contact us at:

Email: webadmin@justask.org.uk Address: Just Ask! Web Administrator, Selborne House, 54-60 Victoria Street, London, SW1A 6QW.

English
Cymraeg
اردو
বাংলা
廣州話
ਪੰਜਾਬੀ
ગુજરાતી

Disclaimer

△ **Top**   **Designed and Powered by iCL**

Above – JustAsk is an innovative online facility of the Community Legal Service (see page 32).
Below – Searching for law-related sites in the popular Yahoo! internet directory (see page 23).

Bookmarks | Location: http://uk.dir.yahoo.com/Regional/Countries/United_Kingdom/Govern

| law | Search | All sites ▾ | advanced search |

All sites
UK sites only
Ireland sites only
This category only

* **Join a Chat**

* **Alternative Dispute Resolution** *(6)*
* **Booksellers@**
* **Cases** *(9)*
* **Companies and Firms@**
* **Consumer** *(4)*
* **Criminal Justice** *(7)*
* **Employment Law** *(3)*
* **Employment Resources** *(2)*
* **Environmental@**
* **Firms@**
* **Health** *(4)*
* **History** *(1)*
* **Immigration and Naturalisation** *(3)*

* **Intellectual Property** *(6)*
* **Journals** *(2)*
* **Law Enforcement@**
* **Law Schools** *(22)*
* **Legal Research** *(6)*
* **Lesbian, Gay and Bisexi Resources@**
* **News and Media** *(9)*
* **Organisations** *(10)*
* **Privacy** *(5)*
* **Self-Help** *(2)*
* **Software Companies@**
* **Web Directories** *(4)*

1 Using the internet

In this chapter we will explore:

▶ *getting started*
▶ *using search engines*
▶ *tips for searching*
▶ *bookmarking your favourite web sites*
▶ *the most popular search engines*
▶ *search utilities*
▶ *newsgroups*
▶ *internet mailing lists*
▶ *using online legal information correctly*

This book seeks to aid and support students studying law by identifying the key legal web sites to support their studies. It is not meant as a substitute for attendance at lectures, seminars, or tutors' reading lists, but it should save you a great deal of time if you are planning to use the internet. This opening chapter sets out some useful legal information sites and well-known search engines.

▶ Chapter 2 presents the major legal institutions' web sites for reference purposes.

▶ Chapter 3 should help you start using the internet as a legal research tool.

▶ Chapter 4 reviews useful core law sites to help you focus on key areas and legal issues.

▶ Chapter 5 shows how and where to access law journals online.

▶ Chapter 6 highlights some useful law students contacts.

▶ Lastly, Chapter 7 examines the British legal profession on the net and provides a directory of law firms, careers, publishers and miscellaneous law sites.

Getting started

Already many UK lawyers have developed web sites offering their services. The courts, too, have seen the widespread introduction of computer technology to assist them. Moreover, many law schools have decided to make use of online learning spaces, or to put handouts on web pages for the benefit of students. These proliferating techniques clearly underline the growing importance of the internet and its increasing acceptance as a legitimate medium in law.

Using the internet ....

Resources to help you
If you are having trouble getting started on the net, you could take a look at other illustrated paperbacks in the Internet Handbooks series including:

Exploring Yahoo! on the Internet, David Holland.

Finding a Job on the Internet, Brendan Murphy (2nd edition).

Getting Started on the Internet, Kye Valongo.

Internet for Students, David Holland (reprinted).

Law & Lawyers on the Internet, Stephen Hardy.

Where to Find It on the Internet, Kye Valongo (2nd edition).

Fig. 1. The home page of Internet Handbooks. The web site offers a range of free help on using the internet.

Or you could explore the following site:

Tutorials for Lawyers
http://www.venables.co.uk/students.htm
Within this substantial site, you will find courses for law students, with major lists of law schools and law courses in the UK. Some of the courses described have particular relevance to the internet. There is a section on careers advice, training contracts and pupillages, and some free CV development services. The 'resources for law students' area includes free case notes and course materials, competitions,

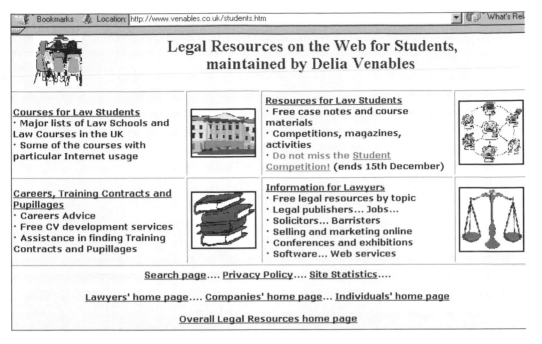

Legal Resources on the Web for Students, maintained by Delia Venables

Courses for Law Students
· Major lists of Law Schools and Law Courses in the UK
· Some of the courses with particular Internet usage

Resources for Law Students
· Free case notes and course materials
· Competitions, magazines, activities
· Do not miss the Student Competition! (ends 15th December)

Careers, Training Contracts and Pupillages
· Careers Advice
· Free CV development services
· Assistance in finding Training Contracts and Pupillages

Information for Lawyers
· Free legal resources by topic
· Legal publishers... Jobs...
· Solicitors... Barristers
· Selling and marketing online
· Conferences and exhibitions
· Software... Web services

Search page.... Privacy Policy.... Site Statistics....

Lawyers' home page.... Companies' home page... Individuals' home page

Overall Legal Resources home page

magazines, and activities. The site is maintained by Delia Venables.

Once you have got started, then try out these sites for fun:

Cyber Law Centre
http://www.cyberlawcentre.org.uk/
This is 'the site that cites intellectual property resources on the net.' According to Internet Magazine: 'The Cyber Law Centre is a collection of legal resources, includes relevant links, mailing lists and research tools, with more to come. One of the most interesting elements is the conference, which seems reasonably active, and this whole site is well on the way to developing into a valuable resource for legal beagles.' The site is maintained by Hannah Oppenheim, a Member of the Computer Law Association and Association of Internet Users.

Fig. 2. Delia Venables' excellent web site contains many useful sets of links for students.

Fig. 3. The Cyber Law Centre.

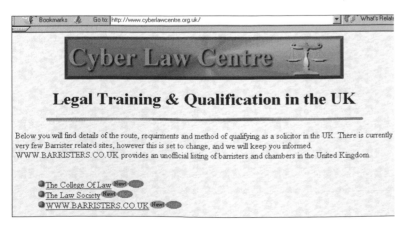

Cyber Law Centre

Legal Training & Qualification in the UK

Below you will find details of the route, requirments and method of qualifying as a solicitor in the UK. There is currently very few Barrister related sites, however this is set to change, and we will keep you informed.
WWW.BARRISTERS.CO.UK provides an unofficial listing of barristers and chambers in the United Kingdom

· The College Of Law *New!*
· The Law Society *New!*
· WWW.BARRISTERS.CO.UK *New!*

Using the internet ....

Law Lounge
http://www.lawlounge.com/main.htm
This web site consists of a mixed bag of legal links combined with a 'cyber lounge'. Information is classified by topic, such as corporate and commercial, personal and social, criminal, public and administrative, international, information and communication. You can read the latest legal news from Europe, Americas and Australia, and explore a full listing of online academic journals plus links to world general and financial newspapers. Law Lounge bulletin boards discuss a range of topical issues including rights and freedoms, internet law, corporate law and criminal law. The site also features a substantial listing of all the American, British, Australian and Canadian law schools and colleges and law student societies.

Injunctions
Legal Aid
Private Housing
Public Housing
Relationships
Small Claims Co

Law Rights
http://www.lawrights.co.uk/
Law Rights is a privately run and funded company that offers free independent legal information for the public in England and Wales. It was formed to provide concise legal information to both consumers and business customers. It has since expanded to offer a range of direct legal services that use the internet to reduce the time and cost normally associated with seeking legal advice. The legal content on Law Rights is written and updated by a team of barristers, solicitors and academics. There are links to areas dealing with accident claims, adoption, case examples, consumer topics, employment law, injunctions, children's law, legal aid, private and public housing, relationships, and the Small Claims Court. You can even access Law Rights legal information from your WAP-enabled mobile phone via Law Rights Mobile.

Using search engines

The usual way to look up something on the internet is to go to the web site of a well-known search engine or internet directory. These services are free and open to everyone.

▶ *Search engines* – These are also known as spiders or crawlers. They have highly sophisticated search tools that automatically seek out web sites across the internet. These trawl through and index literally millions of pages of internet content. As a result they often find information that is not listed in traditional directories.

▶ *Internet directories* – These are developed and compiled by people, rather than by computers. Web authors submit their web site details, and these details get listed in the relevant sections of the directory.

The browser that your ISP supplies you with – typically Internet Explorer or Netscape – should include an internet seach facility, ready for you to use, but you are perfectly free to visit any of the search engines listed below, and use them yourself.

Most people refer to directories as search engines and lump the two together. For the purposes of this book, we will refer to them all as search engines. Popular search engines have now become big web sites in their own right, usually combining many useful features. As well as search boxes where you can type key words to summarise what you are looking for, you will usually also find handy directories of information, news, email and many other services. There are hundreds if not thousands of search engines freely available. The biggest and best known are AltaVista, Excite, Infoseek, Lycos and Yahoo! (the most popular of all).

Tips for searching

1. If you want general information, try Yahoo! or AltaVista first. For specific information, try one or more of the major search engines. After experimenting, many people decide on their own favourite search engine and stick to it most of the time.

2. If you do a search for careers guidance, the search engine will search for 'careers', and search for 'guidance' quite separately. This could produce details of missile guidance, for example – not what you want. The way to avoid this is to enclose all your key words inside a pair of quotation marks. If you type in 'careers guidance' then only web sites with that combination of words should be listed for you.

3. George Boole was a 19th-century English mathematician who worked on logic. He gave his name to Boolean operators – simple words like AND, OR and NOT. If you include these words in your searches, it should narrow down the results, for example: 'careers AND guidance NOT Europe'. However, don't go overboard and restrict the search too much, or you may get few or no results.

4. Try out several different search engines, and see which one you like the best. Or you could obtain the handy little search utility called Web Ferret (see below): if the information is not on one search engine, Web Ferret can usually find it on one or more of the others.

Bookmarking your favourite web sites

Your browser (usually Internet Explorer or Netscape Navigator) enables you to save the addresses of any web sites you specially like, and may want to revisit. These are called Bookmarks in Netscape, or Favorites in Internet Explorer (US spelling). In either case, simply mouse-click on the relevant button on your browser's toolbar – Book-marks or Favorites as the case may be. This produces a little drop-down menu that you click on to add the site concerned. When you want to revisit that site later, click again on the same button; then click the name of the web site you bookmarked, and within a few seconds it should open for you.

The most popular search engines

Bookmarks   Go to: http://www.altavista.co.uk/

Click a tab for more on "law"

The UK Web	The World Wide Web	Images	MP3/Audio

law - Click here for a list of words related to law.

WEB PAGES   ▸ 738920 pages found.

1. The Law Society
......
http://www.lawsociety.org.uk/
Last Modified: 22 May 2000 - 0.6 K - English [Translate] More pages from this site

2. The Law Society
......
http://www.lawsoc.org.uk/
Last Modified: 22 May 2000 - 0.6 K - English [Translate] More pages from this site

3. The College of Law
College of Law......
http://www.lawcol.org.uk/
Last Modified: 4 Aug 2000 - 52.9 K - English [Translate] More pages from this site

Fig. 4. Exploring law links on the UK pages of the Altavista search engine.

AltaVista
http://www.altavista.com
This portal offers specialist research options, as well as text and video. Its results are often US-centric. Alta Vista is one of the most popular search sites among web users world wide. It contains details of many millions of web pages on its massive and ever-growing database. You can either follow the trails of links from its home page, or (better) type in your own key words into its search box. You can even search in about 25 different languages.

Ask Jeeves
http://www.askjeeves.com/
Ask Jeeves offers a slightly different approach to searches. It invites you to ask questions on the internet just as you would of a friend or colleague. For example you could type in something like: 'What is an employment tribunal?' Jeeves retrieves the information, drawing from a growing knowledge base of millions of answers.

Electronic Yellow Pages
http://www.eyp.co.uk
Before the internet, when looking for book information, what did you do? Most people simply opened up their Yellow Pages and started ringing round. Well now in a more sophisticated way you can do this online. These electronic yellow pages are organised much like the printed edition. Just type in the details of the information you need - anything from solicitors to law publishers - and it quickly searches for appropriate services in your local area.

Excite
http://www.excite.com
Excite is another of the top ten search engines and directories on the internet. To refine your search, simply click the check boxes next to the words you want to add and then click the Search Again button. There are separate Excite home pages for several different countries and cultures including Australia, Chinese, France, German, Italy, Japan, Netherlands, Spain, Sweden, and the USA. You will find its dedicated UK site at: http://www.excite.co.uk/

Global Online Directory
http://www.god.co.uk/
Launched in 1996, GOD is fairly unusual among search engines in that it is UK-based, and aims to be a premier European search service. Features of the site include a 'global search' where you can search for web sites by country, state, province, county or even city by city, narrowing down the information and arriving at a more focused result. This is advantageous as the web grows, and as the information thrown up by general search engines becomes ever more over-whelming.

Google
http://www.google.com
A new and innovative search site is Google, which has an easy-to-use no-nonsense format. It matches your query to the text in its index, to find relevant pages. For instance, when analysing a page for indexing, it looks at what the pages linking to that page have to say about it, so the rating partly depends on what others say about it. This highly-regarded search facility has indexed well over a billion pages on the world wide web, and is now helping to power Yahoo!

HotBot
http://hotbot.lycos.com/
This is an impressive, very popular, and well-classified search engine and directory, now associated with Lycos (see below).

Using the internet..

Google™

Advanced Search   Preferences   Search Tips

`law training contracts`

Google Search   I'm Feeling Lucky

Tip: In most browsers you can just hit the return key instead of clicking on the search button.

Searched the web for **law training contracts**.   Results **1 - 10** of about **289,000**. Search took **0.72** seconds.

Hotjobs.com Thousands of Jobs Available   Sponsored Link
www.hotjobs.com   Easy and User-Friendly Approach to Job Hunting

The **Law** Careers Advice Network: Introduction
... When non-**law** graduates should apply for a **training** contract
which will begin September 2002/Spring 2003. ...
www.lcan.csu.ac.uk/Train/Nonlaw.htm - 45k - Cached - Similar pages

The **Law** Careers Advice Network: Introduction
... **Training contracts** - non-**law** graduates, Alternative careers. A career
as a solicitor in commerce and industry, Specialist Bar Associations.
www.lcan.csu.ac.uk/Train/Train.htm - 9k - Cached - Similar pages
[More results from www.lcan.csu.ac.uk]

LAW IMPACT. **LAW** 863.84. **TRAINING CONTRACTS** CONVERTED INTO ...
Capitolo: 03.02.10 Scheda: **LAW** IMPACT. **LAW** 863.84. **TRAINING CONTRACTS** CONVERTED
INTO PERMANENT POSTS Directory: LAVORO/ULMO/IMPAT863/CFLTRASF. ...
www.rer.camcom.it/gc/guida/gui_58.htm - 4k - Cached - Similar pages

Fig. 5. Google has emerged in the last year or two as one of the most respected search engines. Here it is being used to search for web sites dealing with law training contracts.

Infoseek (Go Network)
http://infoseek.go.com/
Infoseek is one of the leading search engines on the internet. In 1994, the American 'netpreneur' Steve Kirsch founded Infoseek with the mission of helping people unleash the power of the internet. He pioneered a suite of powerful, high-quality and easy-to-use search tools which allowed everyone – even those with limited computer skills - to access information online. Infoseek is now part of Disney's Go Network.

Internet Address Finder
http://www.iaf.net/
The IAF is used by millions of web users for searching and finding the names, email addresses, and now Intel Internet videophone contacts, of other users world wide. With millions of addresses it is one of the most comprehensive email directories on the internet. When you register for this free service, you'll be instantly connected to the Finder database – no waiting for processing, or passwords to be sent. You can search for family and friends, colleagues, for the famous, and the not-yet-famous. By registering, you will also enable others to find you. Bear in mind that not everyone gives out their email address, preferring to remain 'ex directory' in order to avoid being bombarded with junk email ('spam').

Internet Public Library
http://www.ipl.org/ref/

The 'Ask-A-Question' service at the Internet Public Library is experimental. They say 'We're doing the best we can with what we've got. Right now, our biggest problem is volume: each day, we receive more questions than we can answer with our current staff resources.' The librarians who work at the IPL Reference Centre are mostly volunteers with other full-time librarian jobs. Your question is received at the IPL Reference Centre and the mail is reviewed once a day and questions are forwarded to a place where all the librarians can see them and answer them. Replies will be sent as soon as possible, advising whether your question has been accepted or rejected. If it has been accepted, you should receive an answer to in a day or two – a week or so if it is a harder question.

Internet Sleuth
http://www.isleuth.com
Internet Sleuth is a metasearch tool with over 3,000 databases to choose from. If you want to find something that may be rare or unusual, this is a great place to start. It is an easy site to use and provides an excellent base-camp from which to explore the web. This kind of site can easily bury you under an avalanche of information, so be specific in your search keywords and phrases.

List of Search Engines
http://www.search-engine-index.co.uk/
This enterprising British site offers a free list of hundreds of search engines, covering all kinds of different topics. There are software search engines, multiple search engines, email and news search engines, web search engines, commercial search engines, word reference and science search, law search, TV, film and music search, image search, technology manufacturers search, and various localised search engines.

Looksmart
http://www.looksmart.com
This is another good directory with a huge number of catalogued sites. You can find it on the Netscape Net Search Page. If your search is not successful, you are redirected to AltaVista.

Lycos
http://www.lycos.com
http://www.lycos.co.uk
Lycos is another of the top ten worldwide web search engines. Lycos is the name for a type of ground spider ('spider' being the term for a type of search engine). It searches document titles, headings, links, and keywords, and returns the first few words of each page it indexes for your search. Founded in 1995, Lycos was one of the earliest search and navigation sites designed to help people find information more easily and quickly on the world wide web. The core technology

Lycos Services

Free SMS
Logos & Ringtones
UK Maps
Win with Lycos   NEW
Holidays Online   NEW
Daily Horoscopes
Lycos Chat
Voice Chat from Mediari
Free Email Services
News
Weather
My Lycos

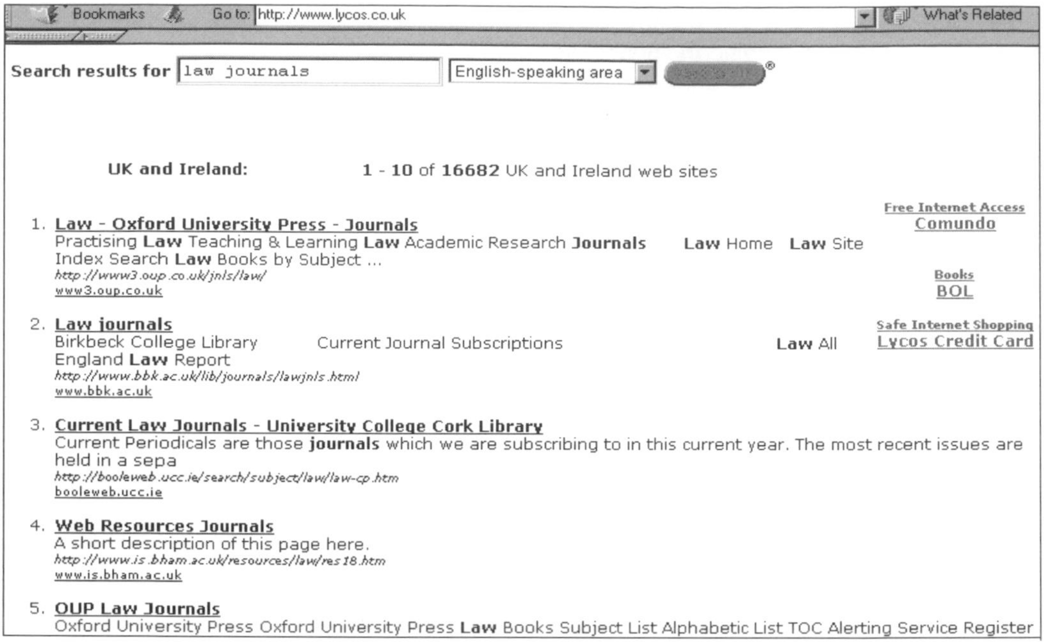

Using the internet..

Fig. 6. Lycos is another of the top search engines, with links to millions of web sites.

was developed at Carnegie Mellon University. Since 1997, with the media giant Bertelsmann, it has launched Lycos sites in 11 European countries.

Metacrawler
http://www.metacrawler.com/
MetaCrawler was originally developed by Erik Selberg and Oren Et-zioni at the University of Washington, and released to the internet in 1995. In response to each user query, it incorporates results from all the top search engines. It collates results, eliminates duplication, scores the results and provides the user with a list of relevant sites.

Metaplus
http://www.metaplus.com/uk.html
Metaplus is a metalist of the best internet directories – and also offers direct links to some key general sites. This is its UK page, containing hundreds of classifications to explore, including UK regional links.

NetSearch
http://www.netsearch.com
NetSearch is one of the original search engines. It is good for email subscription updating services.

SavvySearch
http://www.savvysearch.com/
SavvySearch is one of the leading providers of metasearch services. Its search engine offers a single point of access to more than 200

search engines, guides, archives, libraries, and other resources. Users submit a keyword query which is then immediately and sent out to all appropriate internet search engines. The results are gathered and displayed clearly. SavvySearch has existed as a free internet search service since 1995.

Scoot Yahoo
http://scoot.yahoo.co.uk
Yahoo has combined with the British directory Scoot to offer an excellent search facility for those looking for a whole host of information. Once you have found the organisation you are looking for you can click straight into their web site if they have one.

Search.com
http://search.cnet.com/
This service is run by CNET, one of the world's leading new-media companies. From the home page you can click an A-Z list option which displays an archive of all its search engines. The list is long, but just about everything you need to master the web is there. You can search yellow pages, phone numbers, email addresses, message boards, software downloads, and easily do all kinds of specialty searches.

Search IQ
http://www.searchiq.com/
This site provides reviews of the most popular search engines and directories, including: Altavista, AskJeeves, Excite, Google, Hotbot, Inference, Infoseek, Lycos, and Yahoo. You can use the subject directory to locate what you are looking for quickly. Finding information on the web can be like looking for a needle in a haystack. Speciality search engines are one of the best ways to help you track down the precise information you want.

Starting Point MetaSearch
http://www.stpt.com/search.html
This is a powerful metasearcher that puts over 170 high-quality, popular, and comprehensive search tools - general and category specific – at your fingertips. These tools include AliWeb, AltaVista, Archie, Excite, DejaNews, InfoSeek, Inktomi, Lycos, Netfind, OpenText, SavvySearch, URLsearch,W3 Catalog, WebCrawler, WWWWorm, and Yahoo!

UK Directory
http://www.ukdirectory.co.uk/
Based in Eastleigh near Southampton, this is a useful directory listing to UK-based web sites. You can browse it or search it. It has a well-classified subject listing. UK Directory is simple and intuitive to use. You don't need to know the name of the company, service or person

Legal
• **Conveyancing**
• **Patent Agents**
• **Legal Services**
• **24hr Solicitors**
• **Ombudsman**
• **Bailiffs**
• **Will Writing**
• **Accident Claim**
• **Barristers**

to find the things you are interested in. Just look in the category that best suits your needs. It is as easy to use as a telephone directory.

UK Index
http://www.ukindex.co.uk/
This is another directory of sites in or about the UK. It assigns sites to broad categories to help you with searching.

UK Plus
http://www.ukplus.co.uk/
The parent company of this UK-oriented search engine and database is Daily Mail & General Trust - owners of the Daily Mail, the Mail on Sunday, London Evening Standard and a number of UK regional newspapers – so it draws on a rich tradition of quality publishing. It has built a vast store of web site reviews supplied, not by an unselective computer robot, but by a team of experienced journalists. Although it concentrates on UK web sites of all kinds, you will also find many from all over the world which are included because it feels they are likely to be of interest to British-based readers.

UK Yellow Web Directory
http://www.yell.co.uk/
This site is operated by the yellow pages division of British Telecom. It is indexed 'by humans' and is searchable. A number of non-UK sites are included in the database. There is also an A to Z company listing, but note that companies whose names begin with 'The' are listed under T. A Business Compass lists 'the best' business internet resources, with links and brief descriptions.

Webcrawler
http://webcrawler.com/
Webcrawler is a fast worker and returns an impressive list of links. It analyses the full text of documents, allowing the searcher to locate key words which may have been buried deep within a document's text. Webcrawler is now part of Excite.

World Email Directory
http://www.worldemail.com/
This site is dedicated to email, email, more email, finding people and locating businesses and organisations. WED has access to an estimated 18 million email addresses and more than 140 million business and phone addresses world wide. Here you'll find everything from email software, to email list servers, many world wide email databases, business, telephone and fax directories and a powerful email search engine.

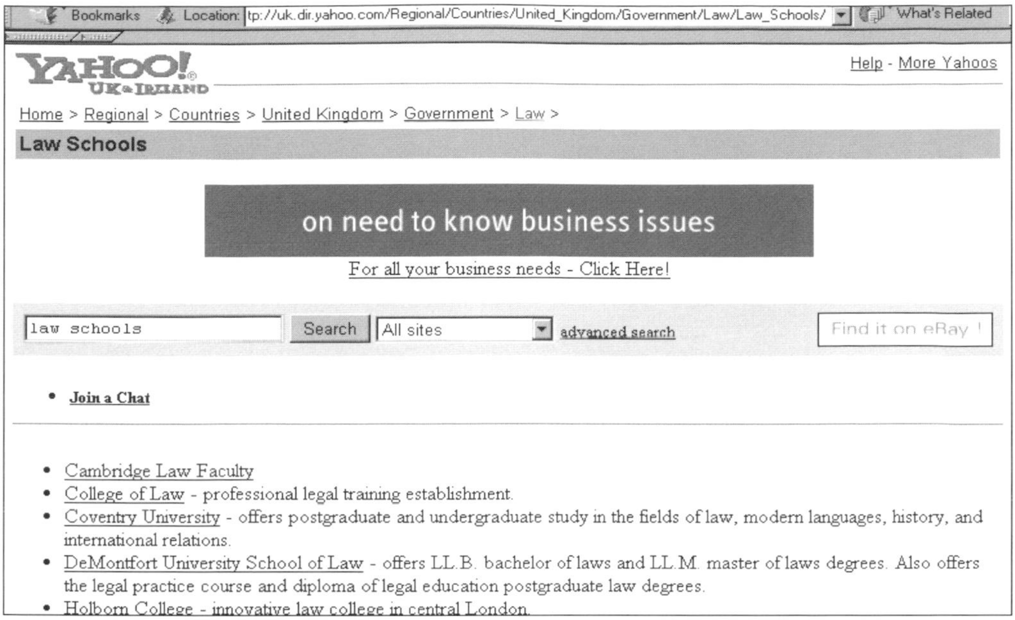

Fig. 7. The Yahoo! search engine and internet directory being used to retrieve a list of the web sites of UK law schools.

Yahoo!

http://www.yahoo.com

http://www.yahoo.co.uk

Yahoo! was the first substantial internet directory, and continues to be one of the best for free general searching. It contains over a billion links categorised by subject. You can 'drill down' through the well-organised categories to find what you want, or you can carry out your own searches using keywords. The site also offers world news, sport, weather, email, chat, retailing facilities, clubs and many other features. Yahoo! is probably one of the search engines and directories you will use time after time, as do millions of people every day.

Search utilities

WebFerret

http://www.ferretsoft.com

WebFerret is an excellent functional search utility. You can key in your query offline, and when you connect it searches the web until it has collected all the references you have specified - up to 9,999 if you wish. WebFerret queries ten or more search engines simultaneously and discards any duplicate results. The search engines it queries include AltaVista, Yahoo, Infoseek, Excite, and others. You can immediately visit the web pages it lists for you, even while WebFerret is still running. The trial version of the program is free, and simplicity itself. It only takes a few minutes to download from FerretSoft. Highly recommended.

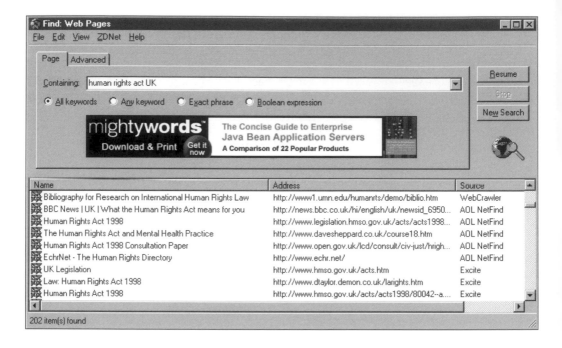

Fig. 8. Web Ferret is a nice alternative to using individual search engines. Just key in your query to Web ferret, and it will search several of the major search engines together, to find you what you want. Here it is being used to search for web sites dealing with the Human Rights Act.

Newsgroups

▶ *Newsgroups* – are public discussion groups freely available on the internet. Each newsgroup is a collection of messages, usually unedited and not checked by anyone ('unmoderated'). Messages can be posted in the newsgroup by anyone including you. The ever-growing newsgroups have been around for much longer than the world wide web and web pages, and are an endless source of good and bad information, news, scandal, entertainment, resources and ideas. The 80,000-plus newsgroups are collectively referred to as Usenet. To access newsgroups, you will need a newsreader – a type of software that enables you to search, read, post, and manage messages in a newsgroup. It will normally be supplied as part of your browser when you first sign up, e.g. Outlook Express (which comes with the Internet Explorer browser), or Messenger (which comes with the Netscape browser).

Deja.com
http://www.deja.com/
Deja.com (originally Deja News) was founded in 1995 as the first web site dedicated exclusively to online discussion, and capable of searching and archiving Usenet newsgroups. With more than six million page views per day, it offers access to millions of messages in more than 45,000 newsgroups. Deja is one of the web's most visited

sites. More than a million people have registered (free) to take advantage of its expanding range of information and community services.

uk.legal

This is an example of a well-known and active UK-based newsgroup, where people – not just lawyers and students - read and post messages about all kinds of legal topics. Some people post using their real names, but many others post anonymously. Don't take all the information at face value. It can be a good place to practise presenting an argument or counter-argument.

Subject	Sender	Date
uk.legal	Total messages: 6374	Unread messages:
Re: Matrix Chambers and Cherie Blair	Paul Hyett	Sat 10:31
Re: Matrix Chambers and Cherie Blair	RDM	Fri 16:17
Re: Matrix Chambers and Cherie Blair	Steve Frazer	Mon 11:58
Re: EU WILL SCRAP ENGLAND ...sorry this is very big.	Robert Henderson	Fri 12:08
Re: Unborn babies have "rights" - Judge	James Hammerton	Fri 14:13
Re: Unborn babies have "rights" - Judge	The Ghost In The Machine	Mon 16:32
Re: Unborn babies have "rights" - Judge	John Savard	Mon 19:13
Re: Unborn babies have "rights" - Judge	John Savard	Mon 19:19
Re: Unborn babies have "rights" - Judge	tbounds@gci.net	Mon 22:09
THE ETHICS OF ABORTION	tewins	08:32
Re: Unborn babies have "rights" - Judge	David	Mon 19:33
Re: Unborn babies have "rights" - Judge	Tim	Mon 21:21
Re: Unborn babies have "rights" - Judge	Stephen Morgan	Mon 23:34
Re: Unborn babies have "rights" - Judge	Cynic	09:40
Re: Unborn babies have "rights" - Judge	John Savard	Mon 19:17
Re: 1 - EU WILL SCRAP BRITAIN & ENGLAND [proof EU maps]	Derek Bell	Fri 13:13
Re: Marriage	Neil	Fri 13:27
Re: Solicitors don't pay/interest law	dave	Fri 14:11
Re: "Free Speech" (Was: Re: Mosney illegal immigrant camp [ca...	Gerard	Fri 13:33
Re: PLEASE - HELP ME	thewiz	Fri 13:44

Accessing particular newsgroups

The normal way to explore newsgroups is to use the newsreading software in your computer – probably Outlook Express, or Netscape Messenger. The very first time you do this, it could take five or ten minutes for your computer to download the names of many thousands of newsgroups available from your news server (probably your ISP). After that, you can usually access any of them at any time in a matter of seconds.

Alternatively, to access the messages in a particular newsgroup, you can just type the address exactly as shown above into your browser's address box: the name of the newsgroup, prefixed by 'news:', for example:

Fig. 9. An example of a newsgroup. This one is called uk.legal. It shows some of the many message headers – over 6,000 in this newsgroup! – some of them shown in 'threads' on the same theme. Just click on any header to read the relevant message.

news:uk.legal

Your newsreading software (Outlook Express or Netscape Messenger), and the messages in the newsgroup, should then open up for you automatically.

Be warned, there could be hundreds or even thousands of messages the first time you access a particular newsgroup, so it could take several minutes for all the headers to be loaded into view. You can then instantly sort them by date, subject, or name of sender. Click on any of the headers (single line descriptions) that take your fancy, and you can then read the message in an adjacent panel.

Some law-related newsgroups
Here is a selection of Usenet newsgroups having some law-related content:

alt.building.law	alt.law.enforcement
alt.law	at.law.war-crimes
alt.lawyers	misc.legal
alt.philosophy.law	misc.legal.computing
alt.uk.law	misc.legal.moderated
clari.news.law	scot.legal
clari.world.law	uk.legal
england.legal	us.legal

Internet mailing lists

▶ *Mailing lists* – In internet parlance, a mailing list is a forum where members can distribute messages by email to the members of the forum, and where all the members ('subscribers') can read the messages posted. There are two types of lists, discussion and announcement. Discussion lists allow exchange of messages between list members. Announcement lists are one-way only and used to distribute information such as news or humour. A good place to look for specific mailing lists is Liszt (see below).

Liszt
http://www.listzt.com
Liszt offers the largest index of mailing lists on the internet. It covers every conceivable area of interest - more than 90,000 lists in all. It also offers a Usenet newsgroups directory and an IRC (internet relay chat) directory. You can obtain a great deal of information here, and network with a very large number of people.

MailBase
http://www.mailbase.ac.uk/
Run from the University of Sheffield, MailBase is the best known and largest source of special interest mailing lists in the UK, over 2,000 in all. You can search its database of lists to find the one(s) that interest you, and then subscribe (free) to read and post messages on that particular academic topic – law, or what you will. It is very popular with lecturers and researchers.

MAILBASE

Beginners

- What is Mailbase?
- What people said
- How to use Mailbase
- List Guidelines

Help Pages

- All Help Pages...
- All about Mailbase...

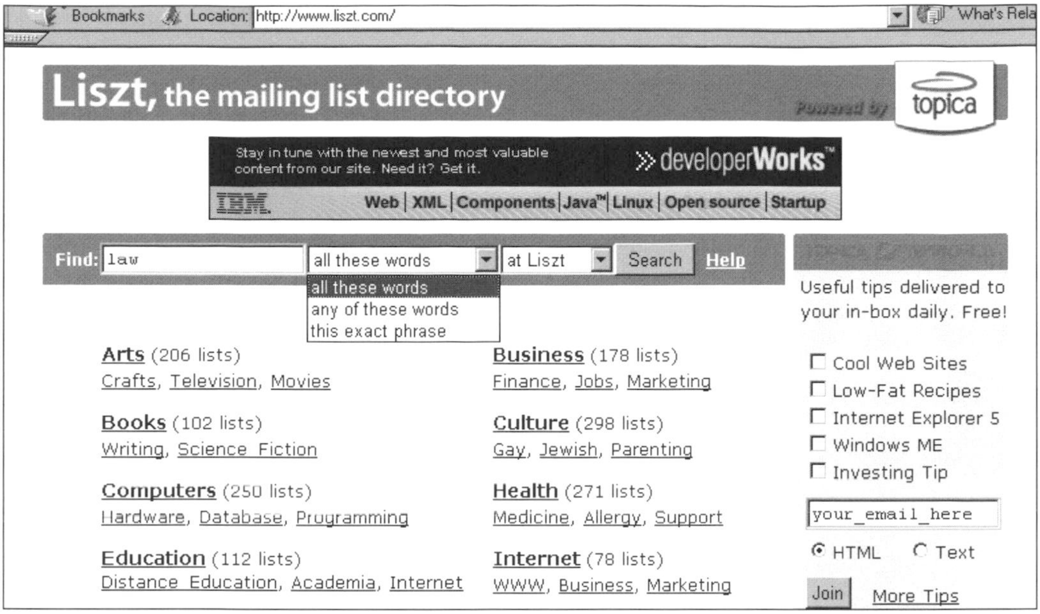

Liszt, the mailing list directory Powered by topica

Stay in tune with the newest and most valuable content from our site. Need it? Get it.
>> developerWorks™

IBM. Web | XML | Components | Java™ | Linux | Open source | Startup

Find: law | all these words ▼ | at Liszt ▼ | Search | Help
all these words
any of these words
this exact phrase

Arts (206 lists)
Crafts, Television, Movies

Books (102 lists)
Writing, Science Fiction

Computers (250 lists)
Hardware, Database, Programming

Education (112 lists)
Distance Education, Academia, Internet

Business (178 lists)
Finance, Jobs, Marketing

Culture (298 lists)
Gay, Jewish, Parenting

Health (271 lists)
Medicine, Allergy, Support

Internet (78 lists)
WWW, Business, Marketing

Useful tips delivered to your in-box daily. Free!

☐ Cool Web Sites
☐ Low-Fat Recipes
☐ Internet Explorer 5
☐ Windows ME
☐ Investing Tip

your_email_here
⦿ HTML ◯ Text
Join More Tips

Using online legal information correctly

Although the publication of law and legal services on the web is a recent innovation, the well-established laws and principles of copyright, usage and liability continue to apply. To that end, students should be vigilant. Information on the net is only claimed to be accurate at the time of posting. Be careful to check the date of the information cited.

You should also reference your web site sources when citing them in your own notes, and especially in essays, assignments or dissertations. Above all, you should not use the internet for purchasing essays! In the first place, they are of a poor quality. Secondly, tutors will very likely detect that they are not the student's own work. Some UK higher education institutions are now using sophisticated software techniques to detect plagiarism by students. You have been warned!

In the next chapter the major legal institutions on the web are presented.

Fig. 10. Liszt is the best-known and biggest source of links to internet mailing lists. These cover every subject under the sun.

2 The major legal institutions

This chapter presents law students with the web sites of the major legal institutions such as parliament, government and the courts. It also examines various law links which will give access to students on a wide range of legal topics. In this chapter we explore the web sites of:

▶ *legal institutions*
▶ *government sites*
▶ *the courts*
▶ *law links*

Legal institutions

The key legal institutions in the UK are the executive, legislature, and judiciary – in plain English the government, the courts and parliament. Below are the British key legal institutions on the web.

Crown Prosecution Service
http://www.cps.gov.uk
Check out this web site for case updates, a news desk, an annual report and other publications.

Lord Chancellor's Department
http://www.open.gov.uk/lcd/lcdhome.htm
This 'gateway' site from the Lord Chancellor's Department (LCD) explains the main departmental role of the Lord Chancellor. This site explains to students that the LCD's function covers the management of the courts, appointment of judges and magistrates, and the administration of legal aid, recent government legislation and reform. In particular, the sections for what's new, press notices and speeches give up-to-date information on what the latest law is.

In addition, the LCD Research site gives information on pending law reform and current recent projects, which is often very useful for law essays. The remainder of this 'gateway' site (so-called because it gives access to related sites) is divided into three: (i) it provides subject legal information (divided into the civil and criminal jurisdictions); (ii) statute law and human rights databases; and (iii), the invaluable 'related links' site which gives access to other government departments and agencies, legislative sources (e.g. Parliament, HMSO, Inquiries, and other useful sites (the Bar Council, Law Society, etc). With access to over fifty other law-related sites, this site cannot be overlooked by law students.

Bookmarks   Location: http://www.open.gov.uk/lcd/lcdhome.htm   What's Related

THE LORD CHANCELLOR'S DEPARTMENT

The Lord Chancellor's main departmental role is to secure the efficient administration of justice in England and Wales. Broadly speaking he is responsible for:

- The effective management of the courts.
- The appointment of judges, magistrates and other judicial office holders.
- The administration of legal aid.
- The oversight of a varied programme of Government civil legislation and reform in such fields as family law, property law, defamation and legal aid.

What's New?	**Press Notices**	**Speeches**
The Department	**The Courts**	**LCD Research**
Legal Aid & Conditional Fees	**Judges and QCs**	**Magistrates**
Civil Matters	**Consultation Papers**	**Criminal Matters**

Fig. 11. The home page of the Lord Chancellor's web site, showing some of the links to further information.

The Government
http://www.open.gov.uk
Another key site for students of any discipline, but especially law, is the UK Government's primary web site. This service provides an accessible entry point to a vast amount of information on the UK public sector. It has both organisation and topic indices, as well as a quick search tool. From this other gateway site you can access all government departments, parliament, public inquiries, royal commissions, local authorities and other public services providers. Its useful What's New page gives valuable insights into the latest new sites available on the web.

House of Lords Judgements
http://www.parliament.the-station.pa/ld199697/ldjudgmnt
This is an essential site for law students. The House of Lords' Judicial Business site provides full transcripts of its judgments delivered by the UK's highest court since 14 November 1996. See also New Law Online which offers access to judgements from the High Court in London, the Court of Appeal, the House of Lords and Privy Council, and the European Court of Justice:

http://www.newlawonline.com/

European Union
http://www.europa.eu.int
The European Union's institutions site gives wide-ranging access to

law. Accessed by eleven different working languages of the EU, gives you access to the major institutions of the EU, including the Council, Parliament, Commission and the European Court of Justice (ECJ). Each institution provides information on the latest EU regulation, policies, and proposed legislative changes. The ECJ site provides access to its case law since 1964, and directly connects to the ECJ's database and researching facilities. See:

http://www.europa.eu.int/cj

The ECJ's case law archive is an exceptionally useful site for law students (figure 6, Curia).

Government sites

As law students will already be aware, apart from these key gateway sites, the government has directed that its departments be accessible to the public. Below are some of its main departments.

The Court Service
http://www.courtservice.gov.uk/
The Court Service is an executive agency of the Lord Chancellor's Department, providing administrative support to a number of courts and tribunals in England and Wales. These include the High Court, the Crown Court and the county courts. Its prime aim is to promote an impartial and efficient operation. While the outcome of cases coming before these courts and tribunals is determined by a judge or a judicial officer, much of the supporting administrative work is carried out by Court Service staff.

Fig. 12. The Court Service is an essential web site for student reference.

The Court Service web site provides a 'map' of the overall court system indicating, in red type, where judgments are already available on the site. This site allows law students access to all the higher courts within the UK from the comfort of your own desk. Long gone are the days of having to go down to your local courts (though always worth a visit . . .). Now, you can access the national courts from your computer:

The Home Office
http://www.homeoffice.gov.uk
They say: 'The Home Office is the government department responsible for internal affairs in England and Wales. The principal aim of the Home Office is to build a safe, just and tolerant society in which the rights and responsibilities of individuals, families and communities are properly balanced and the protection and security of the public are maintained.' The site is a source of press releases, research data, publications and legislation, for example in the fields of constitutional and community issues, human rights, race equality, freedom, of information, data protection, elections, political parties and European issues, and criminal justice.

Home Office
BUILDING A SAFE, JUST AND TOLERANT SOCIETY

▷ **WHAT'S NEW**
▷ **Press Releases**
▷ **Legislation**
▷ **Public Appointments**
▷ **Organisation**
▷ **Aims**
▷ **HOW TO guides**

Legal Aid and the Legal Services Commission
http://www.open.gov.uk/lab/legal.htm
The Legal Aid site informs people about: who can apply, income limits and how to get it. It is very useful for statistical data. Publicly funded legal services in England and Wales are now administered by the Legal Services Commission (LSC). Information about the Commission, its work and the current funding scheme can be found on its web site at:

www.legalservices.gov.uk

The Legal Services Commission was created under the Access to Justice Act 1999 to develop and administer two schemes in England and Wales:

1. The Community Legal Service, which replaces the old civil scheme of legal aid, bringing together networks of funders such as local authorities and suppliers into partnerships to provide the widest possible access to information and advice.

2. The Criminal Defence Service which from April 2001 replaces the old system of criminal legal aid and provide criminal services to people accused of crimes.

Legal Services Commission
http://www.legalservices.gov.uk/
The Legal Services Commission is a new executive non-departmental public body which exists to develop and administer two schemes

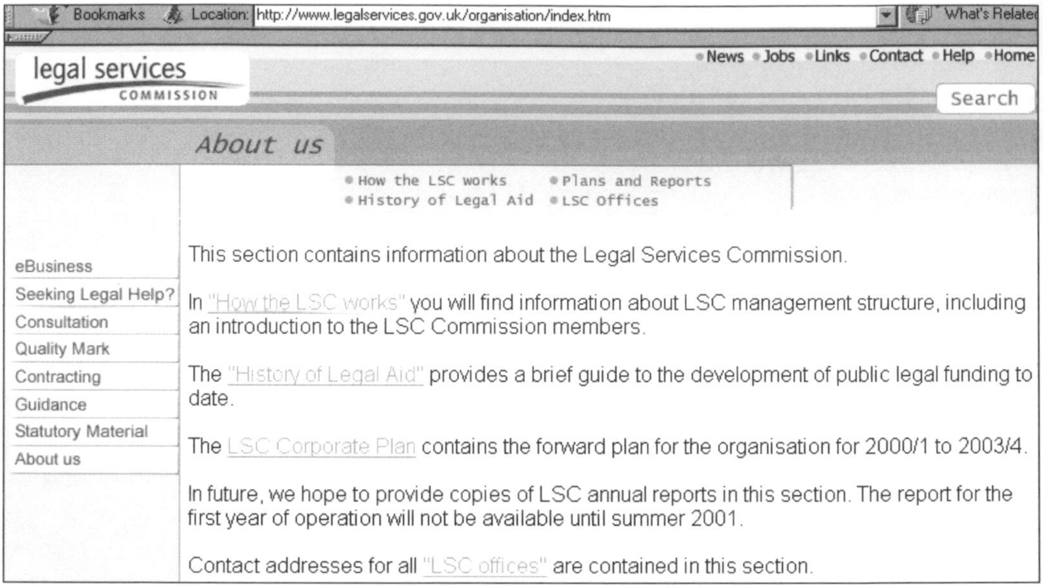

The major legal institutions ....

Fig. 13. The Legal
Services Commission.

in England and Wales: (1) The Community Legal Service, which replaces the old civil scheme of legal aid, bringing together networks of funders (e.g. local authorities) and suppliers into partnerships to provide the widest possible access to information and advice. (2) The Criminal Defence Service, provides criminal services to people accused of crimes and its web site is a source of statutory material and guidance.

The www.justask.org.uk site launches the web site of the Community Legal Service which heralds a new era in the use of the internet to improve access to justice. In eight different languages this new site offers a directory of solicitors (some 15,000 in total) and an advice search facility (with over 300 linked sites). Will it become the UK citizen's first port of call whenever they have a legal problem? We will have to wait and see ...

The Official Solicitor
http://www.offsol.demon.co.uk/
As law students should be aware, the Office of Official Solicitor provides representation for persons under legal disability (and others) in county court or High Court proceedings in England and Wales. The Official Solicitor is guardian ad litem or next friend of last resort. His office can be traced back to medieval times since the state has always recognised need for representation of an incapacitated person when a benevolent relative or friend cannot be found to act on his behalf. This site gives both technical and practical information for the legal profession, and for members of the general public. Some important changes take effect from 1 April 2001, and information about this is available here.

The court system in the UK is both complex and hierarchical. However, the advent of computer technology in court – even if only to print off DVLA print outs for road traffic offenders – marks progress. The courts are clearly utilising technology more and more. In the next section we will look at courts on the web.

The courts

As noted above, the Court Service's web site offers selected judgments, practice directions, forms and leaflets. See also:

The Court of Appeal (Civil Division)
http://www.courtservice.gov.uk/notices/civil/not_civil.htm
This is the Court Service's site for the Court of Appeal (Civil Division). It includes a court guide and notices and a review of the legal year.

The Court of Appeal (Criminal Division)
http://www.courtservice.gov.uk/notices/crim/not_crim.htm
This is the Court Service's site for the Court of Appeal (Criminal Division). It includes notices, and a guide to proceedings.

The High Court
http://www.courtservice.gov.uk/
This is the Court Service's site with links to the Queen's Bench Division, Admiralty Court, Commercial Court, Crown Office, the Technology & Construction Court, Chancery Division, Patents Court, Family Division and other services.

Fig. 14. The Judges web site. Here you can view a list of the senior judiciary, their current salary scales, training, judgments, speeches, information about Queen's Counsel, and much more.

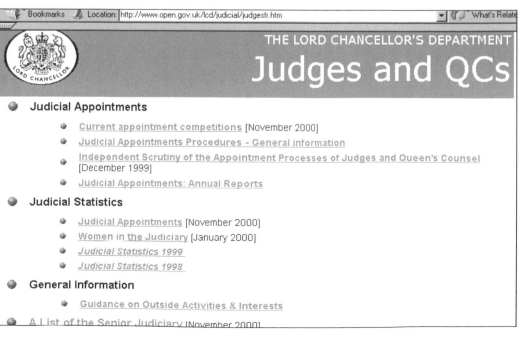

THE LORD CHANCELLOR'S DEPARTMENT
Judges and QCs

- **Judicial Appointments**
  - Current appointment competitions [November 2000]
  - Judicial Appointments Procedures - General information
  - Independent Scrutiny of the Appointment Processes of Judges and Queen's Counsel [December 1999]
  - Judicial Appointments: Annual Reports
- **Judicial Statistics**
  - Judicial Appointments [November 2000]
  - Women in the Judiciary [January 2000]
  - Judicial Statistics 1999
  - Judicial Statistics 1998
- **General Information**
  - Guidance on Outside Activities & Interests
  - A List of the Senior Judiciary [November 2000]

Location: http://www.open.gov.uk/lcd/judicial/judgesfr.htm

The major legal institutions ....

The Judges
http://www.open.gov.uk/lcd/judicial/judgesfr.htm
This site provides information on HM judges – how to apply, who they are, their salaries, and the office. In particular there are links to judicial appointments, current appointment competitions, judicial appointments procedures, general information and annual reports, judicial statistics, guidance on outside activities and interests, a list of the senior judiciary, judicial salary scales, judgments, speeches by senior judges and information about the legal year. This is a very useful resource for writing essays on the judges, as well as Professor Griffith's critique of the judiciary.

```
Who Are Lay Magist
History
Current Numbers
On The Bench
Duties And Respon:
Employing A Magist
Magistrates' Sittings
On The Supplement
Stipendary Magistra
```

Magistrates' Association
http://www.magistrates-association.org.uk
The Magistrates' Association is a registered UK charity. It is the body which represents the 30,000 magistrates – justices of the peace – as they are more commonly known, in England and Wales. This new web site provides general information on how to become a magistrate, about what JPs do, and Magistrates in the Community. It also features a members' page to exchange ideas and provoke discussion. Again, this is a good site for students searching for essay material on the judiciary.

Law links

In the final part of this chapter, we review some law links and portal sites. Law links give students wider opportunity to expand their knowledge beyond single contact web sites. For instance, if you were looking up the Law of Tort, a law link site with cover all civil liability not only tortious ones. See further examples below; many of these are law libraries.

British and Irish Legal Information Institute
http://www.bailii.org
The site offers comprehensive and searchable access to freely available British and Irish public legal information including cases and legislation. As at October 2000, BAILII included 19 databases covering 5 jurisdictions. The system contains over two gigabytes of legal materials and well over 250,000 searchable documents with about 5.5 million hypertext links.

Criminal Justice System
http://www.criminal-justice-system.gov.uk
This UK government web site is a good source of links to the various criminal justice departments, and a selection of publications.

Institute of Advanced Legal Study
http://www.ials.sas.ac.uk
Like the Institute of Advanced Legal Study in Russell Square,

London, itself, this law link site provides an online legal library with a wealth of both national and international legal resources. This is very useful for all law students, especially postgraduate. Its range of materials covers most international jurisdictions. Excellent for students!

Internet Law Library
http://law.house.gov/
This site presents an internet law library, containing various legal commentaries and reports. Law students cannot afford to miss this opportunity.

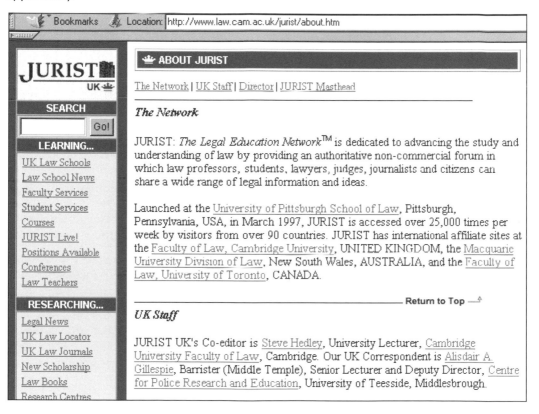

Jurist
http://www.law.cam.ac.uk/jurist/about.htm
This web site gives wide access to students to the latest critical thinking by leading UK law academics. Definitely worth a read! Jurist is the Law Professors' Network, hosted by Cambridge University's Law Faculty. It provides an excellent research tool. It has research data, including law journals, online articles and topic/country guides; and, teaching tools, including UK law schools listings, and discussion pages for both academics and students. It also has legal news pages which cover both the UK and the rest of the world (e.g. the US Supreme Court, and Australian legal news). You will also find the latest law reports from the British courts, International Court, and

Fig. 15. The Jurist web site is a useful law portal for the UK, USA, and other parts of the English-speaking world.

The major legal institutions

the European Courts of Justice and Human Rights. Jurist proclaims itself as 'a clearing house of academically-authored and quality-controlled UK legal resources provided for the convenience of law teachers, law students, lawyers and members of the public in Great Britain and Northern Ireland.'

What's New

About the Law Commiss

Administrative Justice

Common Law

Criminal Law

Property and Trust Law

Statute Law

Law Commission for England and Wales
http://www.lawcom.gov.uk/misc/about.htm
The Law Commission is the independent body set up by Parliament in 1965 (along with a similar Commission for Scotland) to keep the law of England and Wales under review and to recommend reform when it is needed. At any one time the Commission is engaged on between 20 and 30 projects of law reform, at different stages of completion. A typical project will begin with a study of the area of law in question, and an attempt to identify its defects. Foreign systems of law will be examined to see how they deal with similar problems. The Law Commission's site gives details of the latest and archive law reform papers and consultation documents available. It also has details of its latest research programmes. It is another useful tool for tackling essays which ask about law reform.

Law Links
http://www.ukc.ac.uk/library/lawlinks/
Law Links is an excellent annotated list of web sites compiled by Sarah Carter at the University of Kent at Canterbury. Well worth a look.

Lexicon
http://www.courtservice.gov.uk/lexicon/index.htm
Lexicon is a web site from the Court Service giving easy access to selected legal information online. It has been designed for the judiciary of England and Wales to be their primary source of online legal information. Its main focus is to provide access to information relevant to the introduction of the Human Rights Act which came into force in October 2000. The legal links have been structured to give anyone access to legal information on the following areas of law: the United Kingdom, human rights, European and international. The links within each of these areas have been further categorised into current awareness, legislation and treaties, case law, commentary, and organisations. Each link is presented as a descriptive title accompanied by a brief summary to help you determine whether the web site contains the information you are looking for.

Northern Ireland Court Service
http://www.nics.gov.uk/pubsec/courts/courts.htm
Check out this site for the Courts' charter and various other publications. A number of these are available online in PDF format.

Scottish Court Service
http://www.scotcourts.gov.uk
This site provides a useful access point to information relating to all
civil and criminal courts within Scotland. These include the Court of
Session, the High Court of Justiciary, the Sheriff Courts and a number
of other courts, commissions and tribunals as well the District Courts.
The information includes location details, contact numbers, advice
and details of recent significant judgments. The site is regularly updated.

Scottish Law Commission
http://www.scotlawcom.gov.uk/
The Scottish Law Commission is an independent body established
by the Law Commissions Act of 1965. In choosing areas of work the
Commission is guided by judges, lawyers, government departments,
the Scottish Administration and the general public who provide information of their experiences in applying a particular area of the law
or in obtaining legal remedies. The Commission's web site publications page contains the full texts of all discussion papers and reports
published since September 2000. This includes its current sixth programme of law reform and its 34th Annual Report which gives an
overview of its recent work. You can browse or download any of
this material.

▶ *Your legal research* – Lastly, to start you thinking about your future legal research, explore the Findlaw and Infolaw sites:

Findlaw
http://www.findlaw.com
Launched in 1995, Findlaw is a legal search engine powered by Alta
Vista. It is a leading international web portal focused on law and
government, and provides access to a comprehensive and fast-
growing online library of legal resources for use by legal professionals,
consumers and small businesses. Its mission is to make legal information on the internet easy to find. A broad array of features includes
web search utilities, cases and codes, legal news, mailing lists, message boards and free email. It is very useful as a starting point of
access. There are some community boards for discussion of topics
such as greedy associates, divorce, employment law, immigration
law, copyright law, cyberspace law, and personal injury.

Infolaw
http://www.infolaw.co.uk
Infolaw considers legal resources by topic – ADR, arbitration, arts,
Australia, aviation, banking, books, building and construction, business and finance, Canada, cases, civil liberties, commercial law
generally, companies, computer and communications, conferences
and seminars, constitution, consumer, courts, criminal, data bank,

Legal Professionals

Legal Subjects
Constitutional, Intel. Prop., La

CLE Online
Elim. Bias, Ethics, Substance

Lawyer Jobs
Listings, Placement, Submit

Lawyer Marketing
Advertising, Ethics, Strategies

Law Office & Practice
MY FindLaw, Free E-mail, Fre

Software & Technology
Case Management, Time Bill

Consultants & Experts
Referral Services, Witnesses

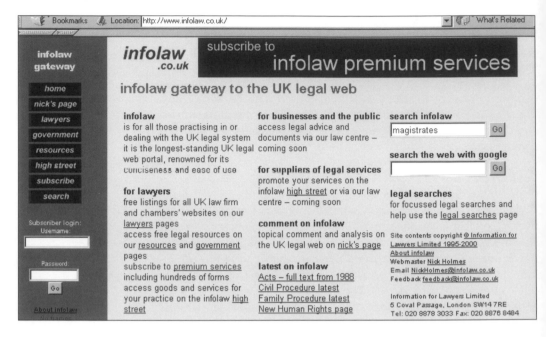

Fig. 16. Infolaw claims to be the longest-standing UK legal web portal. It is an online service maintained by Information for Lawyers Ltd.

data protection, directories, employment, energy, entertainment, environment, equine, Europe, expert witnesses, family, food, forms and precedents, general resources, government, Hong Kong, housing, human rights, immigration, insolvency, insurance, intellectual property, international, internet, Ireland, Jersey, legislation, librarianship, marine, mental health, military, New Zealand, parliament, personal injury, profession, property and conveyancing, Scotland, self help, students and careers, taxation, trade, trusts and estates, welfare and benefits. Again, this is another useful site for students to start from, as it gives an A-Z of law.

In the next chapter, we will examine how to use the net as a legal research tool.

More Internet Handbooks to help you

The Internet for Students, David Holland.
Law & Lawyers on the Internet, Stephen Hardy.
Where to Find It on the Internet, Kye Valongo (2nd edition)

3 Researching on the internet

Are days in the law library over? Or has the virtual law library arrived? This chapter introduces some web sites which will help you to trace case law and find legislation on the internet. As the usage of the web increases, so more and more electronic law reporting and publishing is emerging. In this chapter we review web sites dealing with:

- ▶ *legislation on the net*
- ▶ *how to trace case law*
- ▶ *law reporting*
- ▶ *legal news pages*
- ▶ *legal journals*
- ▶ *miscellaneous*

Legislation on the net

Law students, like lawyers and the judges, spend hours examining the fine intricacies of Statute law, which remains the primary source of UK law. The following sites not only provide access to the Acts of Parliament, but some also provide useful commentaries:

Butterworths
http://www.butterworths.co.uk
Butterworths, the well-known law publishers, host a free online legal newspaper. Their site also contains a Student Notebook, together with student titles, online ordering, case notes, a tour of UK universities, links to other sites and a competition. More importantly for the

Fig. 17. Butterworths is one of the top UK law publishers and information providers.

practitioner are the links to a wide variety of jurisdictions, and various journals. For example:

1. New Law Journal Online, an electronic version of the legal journal.

2. Halsbury's Laws Direct, an online subscription version of Halsbury's Laws of England.

3. All England Direct – includes online subscription access to the All England Law Reports 1936 to date.

4. Law Direct, a current awareness product.

5. The Progress of Legislation database.

6. The Practice Directions database supplies full text of all new Practice Directions within a few hours of issue.

7. The EC Brief service, structured into practice areas and sub-categories.

All will be familiar to law students.

Context
http://www.justis.com
Context is primarily a publisher of CDs, with the online services intended mainly for updating purposes rather than as separate online services. However, for completeness, here are some of the main CD services:

1. Justis Celex – the full text of all treaties, legislation and judgments of the European Court of Justice.

2. Electronic Law Reports, 130 years of The Law Reports on 2 CD-ROMs.

3. Justis Weekly Law, the full archive of The Weekly Law Reports from 1953.

4. Lloyds Electronic Law Reports – commercial, maritime, insurance and reinsurance case law from 1919.

5. The Common Market Law reports – the full text of European Community law reports from 1962. Updated five days a week.

The Stationery Office
http://www.hmso.gov.uk/acts.htm
In the past students would trek to their nearest HMSO shop and

---

Bookmarks   Netsite: http://www.hmso.gov.uk/acts/acts2000.htm

Acts of the UK Parliament 2000

Public Acts

- Northern Ireland Act 2000 c.1
- Representation of the People Act 2000 c.2
- Consolidated Fund Act 2000 c.3
- Armed Forces Discipline Act 2000 c.4
- Nuclear Safeguards Act 2000 c.5
- Powers of Criminal Courts (Sentencing) Act 2000 c.6
- Electronic Communications Act 2000 c.7
- Financial Services and Markets Act 2000 c.8
- Appropriation Act 2000 c.9
- Crown Prosecution Inspectorate Act 2000 c.10
- The Terrorism Act 2000 c.11
- Limited Liability Partnerships Act 2000 c.12
- Royal Parks (Trading) Act 2000 c.13
- Care Standards Act 2000 c.14

---

spend lots of money on buying copies of Statutes. The Stationery Office – formerly the HMSO, the Queen's official publishers – publishes on its site the full texts of Acts as enacted from January 1996. This site makes a very useful starting point for tracing the latest version of Acts. Also, this site contains a list of the Bills currently before Parliament, another useful means of monitoring future legal changes. This is an excellent online resource for students.

The Stationery Office: Statutory Instruments
http://www.hmso.gov.uk/stat.htm
As with the above-mentioned site for Acts, this site conveniently only covers the increasing number of statutory instruments, providing their full texts from 1997.

How to trace case law

Traditionally, every law student has had to endure hours in the law library seeking out law reports. However, the world wide web is changing this. Notably, many law publishers now publish law reports online. This makes finding cases much easier:

Butterworths Law Reporting Service
http://www.butterworths.co.uk/content/aller/index.htm
This is the home of the Butterworths Law Reporting Service, a

Fig. 18. The Stationery Office publishes the complete texts of Acts of Parliament on its web site. Here are just a few of the Acts passed in 2000. Click on any of these links and you can read the full text.

chargeable service which contains the All England Law Reports and other law reports. Student rates are sometimes available. A free trial is available.

Court Service
http://www.courtservice.gov.uk
As mentioned in previous chapters, the government's court service web site contains access to selected Court of Appeal and High Court judgments. The House of Lords dedicated site, referred to in chapter 2, presents transcripts of Lords decisions since November 1996.

European Court of Justice law Reports
http://www.europa.eu.int
This hyperlink site gives access to the ECJ's law reports, as discussed earlier in chapter 2.

Law reporting

Sometimes case law can be hard to track down and students have to resort to transcripts. In such cases, see:

Law Reports (Incorporated Council of Law Reporters)
http://www.lawreports.co.uk
This site from the Incorporated Council of Law Reporters, the official court reporters, gives you wide-ranging access to all courts' transcripts.

Times Law Reports
http://www.the-times.co.uk/
This site offers students the Times Law Reports, including an archive service.

Smith Bernal Law Reports
http://www.smithbernal.com/casebase_frame.htm
Smith Bernal is a well-known and established law reporting provider. It maintains an online law library. Its web site also contains a free database of Court of Appeal judgments since April 1996.

You can also find some of the following case-tracking services helpful:

Lawtel
http://www.lawtel.co.uk
Lawtel, the long established provider of online legal services has offered, by way of subscription unlimited access to all the databases described below, excluding company searches, full text document delivery and new research bureau questions. Students should be warned that these services are available by subscription only. Your law school may corporately subscribe to them. The subscription services available are:

Previous Page

Case No: 2000/2250/A2

IN THE SUPREME COURT C
COURT OF APPEAL (DIVIS
FROM)

Royal Courts of Justice
Strand, London, WC2A 2LL

Date: 18th December 2000

B e f o r e :

THE MASTER OF THE ROL
LORD JUSTICE MAY
and
LORD JUSTICE LAWS

Fig. 19. Lawtel is a useful source of online case reports.

1. Daily Update – a current awareness service with summaries on all legal developments every 24 hours. There are several ways in which this can be received: (i) a full daily update in all areas of law, (ii) personal daily updates customised to focus on any number of specialities, (iii) an email service with full or personal updates, emailed to as many individuals within a law firm as required, and (iv) an online daily update service consisting of full or customised updates, generated online daily.

2. Case Law – cases available within 24 hours of judgment being given. Sources include: House of Lords, Privy Council, Court of Appeal, High Court, QBD: Commercial/Admiralty/ Official Referees/ Divisional Court/Chancery Division/Family Division; Inferior Courts & Tribunals including: Employment Appeal Tribunal, VAT and Duties Tribunal, Lands Tribunal. Lawtel adds the appropriate reference if a case is subsequently reported elsewhere e.g. TLR, AER, WLR. It also covers hundreds of unreported cases each month.

3. Any official judgment from any court, plus advance ordering service; a new tracking service: locates any transcript; personal injury (including quantum); legislation: commencements, repeals, and amendments; statutory instruments; statutes; Parliamentary Bills; Green and White Papers.

4. European Law – an online service for every EU document published since 1987. It offers full text delivery of any official legal document produced by the Communities since 1953.

5. Articles Index (25 major and specialist journals) with hypertext links to relevant cases and legislation.

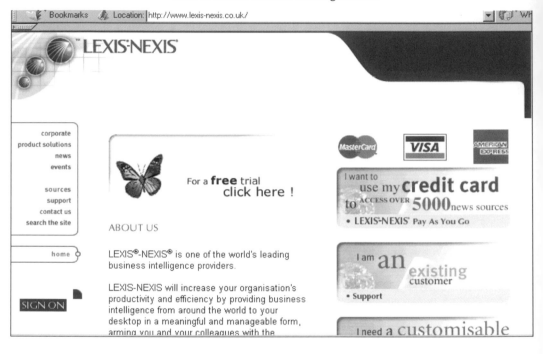

Fig. 20. The home page of the massive Lexis-Nexis web site.

Lexis

http://www.lexis-nexis.co.uk

Lexis was for many years unrivalled in its electronic legal retrieval systems (I recall as a law student myself that this was the only research engine available. How times change!) Some would say it was the forerunner to the world wide web for law. Now modernised and updated, it provides daily free news and updates on: the European Court of Human Rights, the European Monetary Union, and European Investment News. Its non-US legal databases are not yet available in the UK through the internet, although this will come. Subscribers wishing to access the large collections of full text primary source legal materials must in the meantime use the special online service (i.e. not on the web as such). News and business products via the web are already available. These include:

1. European requester – a search service for news sources on companies, products, markets, competitors and people.
2. Tracker – a service to deliver daily targeted information directly to the professional's desktop.

3. Infotailor – a personal daily briefing service consisting of news and information.

4. Tell Me More – a service which connects your web site to selected articles from the Lexis-Nexis services. These articles can then be retrieved by your customers who want to know more about a particular topic. Students should note that free trials are available.

Casebase and Casetrack
http://www.smithbernal.com
Smith Bernal, official reporters to the Courts of Appeal, have recently launched two internet services: Casebase, which is free, and Casetrack, a subscription service.

1. Casebase is an archive of Court of Appeal and Crown Office cases from April 1996 to '30 days ago'. Full texts of all Court of Appeal and Crown Office cases can be viewed or printed out as required. There is an archive comprising more than 20,000 judgments. New judgments are added 30 days after approval. 600+ cases are added each month. Transcripts are searchable by case name, date of judgment, and case number. Court texts are for personal use only. They may not be used, sold or passed on for commercial gain.

2. The Casetrack subscription service provides a listing, tracking, alerting and full text transcript service for all Court of Appeal and Crown Office cases. There are key details of all Court of Appeal and Crown Office cases as listed. Core information is provided about each judgment on the day of judgment. Each case is classified according to key subject area. You can track through the judgment and approval process. Each judgment is classified and fully searchable by name, date, court, the court from which the case has been appealed, judge, subject and counsel. Full texts of transcripts are attached as soon as the approved judgment is available. There is unlimited access to view, print and download any transcript as required. There is full classification of all judgments started from January 1998 onwards. Archived cases from April 1996 will also be accessible through the Casetrack service.

Legal news

In seeking the latest legal news, the internet can be a useful study resource, although newspapers (all now on web) remain a useful information point. Below are some examples from the legal press:

Law Society's Gazette
http://www.lawgazette.co.uk

Researching on the internet...

Bookmarks   Location: http://www.lawgazette.co.uk/homeframe.asp

collected | search this issue [＿＿＿＿＿] go ▸▸ law gazette.co.uk

● breaking news   ● job search   ● search the archive

news

features

opinions

gazette
in practice

customise
the site

legal links

Main news

Judge warns lawyers over costs claim cases

Litigation solicitors were this week chastised by one of the
countryÕs most senior costs judges for misusing costs procedures
introduced by Lord WoolfÕs civil justice reforms last year. collect

General

Double reward for cutting Edge ADR

Hammond Suddards Edge, BNFL and the Independent Housing
Ombudsman scheme last week scooped the fourth biennial
awards from the Centre for Dispute Resolution (CEDR) for
developing alternative dispute resolution (ADR). collect

Cash lifeline as CPS tackles disclosure rules

The government has injected a Õsubstantial Õ sum into
prosecution activities to ensure the Crown Prosecution Service
(CPS) and police can cope with the extra burden of disclosure
obligations introduced last week. collect

ntl:
The complete
communications
company

**PEAPOD
SOLUTIONS
LTD**

**Experts In
Legal I.T.**

Chadwick Nott

Fig. 21. The web site of
the Law Society
Gazette.

This site presents the Law Society's Gazette online, a useful information site for the budding lawyer.

The Lawyer Magazine
http://www.the-lawyer.co.uk
The Lawyer magazine online provides the entire content of each
weekly issue. It also has search facilities that will retrieve stories or
features over the last three years. Legal vacancies are also offered for
those students looking for employment opportunities.

Legalease
http://www.icclaw.com
Legalease – the International Centre for Commercial Law and IT+-
Communications – was the first legal publisher to offer online
services, first of all (several years ago) with LINK and subsequently
with the International Centre for Commercial law. This is one of the
largest and most comprehensive legal sites in Europe with over
60,000 pages. In particular this online publication offers a Student
Law Centre. This offers a free search facility that enables law students
to find details of both law firms offering training contracts and barristers' chambers offering pupilages. You can specify criteria such as
region, work area and start year. A free extensive editorial section is
produced in collaboration with a range of law firms, drawing on the
resources and experience of Legal Business magazine, a leading
magazine for lawyers. There is free advice about preparing a curricu-

lum vitae, guidance on interview techniques, and information about timetables for qualifying as either a solicitor or barrister. Free topical legal updates are issued. There is also a 'behind the scenes' look at training at a range of different size law firms and barristers' chambers.

New Law Journal
http://www.butterworths.co.uk/content/nlj
This site offers selected articles from the more recent New Law Journal. Remember, the NLJ covers topical issues.

Solicitor's Journal
http://www.smlawpub-holborn.co.uk/lawbrief
This site offers the weekly Solicitor's Journal, updated by topic.

Sweet and Maxwell
http://www.smlawpub.co.uk
Sweet and Maxwell is a well established firm of law publishers. Its web site now incorporates the previous FTLaw & Tax site. The intention is to amalgamate the services but at the moment, there are two sets of buttons – the left-hand set (Swiss Cottage) being the original S&M services and the right-hand set (Holborn) being the FT&L set. To locate the services below, you have to look partly in the what's new and internet services on the left-hand side and partly in the free online products on the right. Free services include:

> **Vol 151, No 6968**
>
> click here for
> full journal contents
>
> ---
>
> this week ▪
>
> back issues ▪
>
> subscribe ▪
>
> classified ▪

1. The Badger Alerter. Every day hundreds of documents are issued from Whitehall, Westminster and the Judiciary announcing changes to legislation, new regulations, SIs, decisions, codes of practice and proposals for consultation. This service lists and briefly abstracts every document each day concerning developments of a significant nature, including marked reinforcement or weakening of a legal concept.

2. Law Brief and Case Reports taken from the Solicitors Journal. These are grouped under subject headings and list the source of the report.

3. Electronic newsletters: European Union News Online – Local Government Library. Online – Planning Bulletin Online. Lists from all the Crown Courts in England and Wales, published daily.

4. Case of the Week. Case digests are taken from Current Law, European Current Law, and Hong Kong C L. The Student section has 'Inter-Nutcases' – various case digests of special interest to students, which are very good.

Researching on the internet...

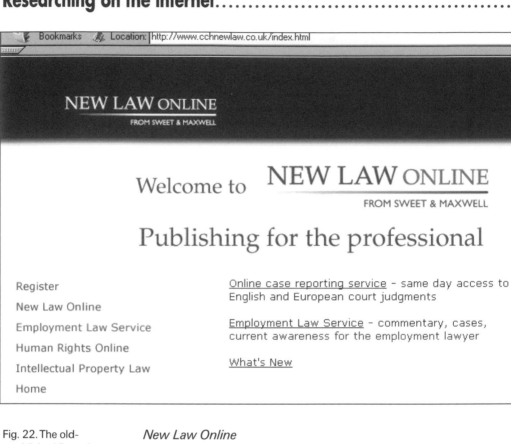

Bookmarks   Location: http://www.cchnewlaw.co.uk/index.html

NEW LAW ONLINE
FROM SWEET & MAXWELL

Welcome to   **NEW LAW** ONLINE
FROM SWEET & MAXWELL

Publishing for the professional

Register

New Law Online

Employment Law Service

Human Rights Online

Intellectual Property Law

Home

Online case reporting service – same day access to English and European court judgments

Employment Law Service – commentary, cases, current awareness for the employment lawyer

What's New

Fig. 22. The old-established firm of Sweet & Maxwell publishes a large range of materials for both student lawyers and practising lawyers, with much information now available online.

New Law Online
http://www.cchnewlaw.co.uk/index.html
New Law Publishing and offers two types of subscription: online and digest. Both cover all areas of law (except family and immigration) in the High Court, Court of Appeal, Privy Council, House of Lords, European Court of Justice, Official Referees' Court and Employment Appeal Tribunal. Online subscribers receive three services in one:

1. Daily digests of important English and European Court decisions on the same day as judgment (as above).

2. Full text reports of those decisions.

3. A rapidly growing and easily searchable database. There are more than 4,000 judgments on the system and this number grows daily. Principal benefits are: speed, selection using defined criteria, reliability and ease of use.

Legal journals

Some law publishers place extracts of legal journals on the net. As mentioned above, the Jurist site gives access to some journals. Also, see chapter 4 for core law curriculum sites of interest to students. However, to date only one journal is web-based:

Current Legal Issues
http://www.ncl.ac.uk/~nlawwww/
The web journal of Current Legal Issues is the first UK web law journal. Its focus is on current legal issues in judicial decisions, law reform, legislation, legal research, policy related socio-legal research, legal information, information technology and practice.

Legal Week
http://www.lwk.co.uk/
Legal Week is an online legal newspaper. It publishes legal news, details of upcoming events, appointments, and a database of UK law firm newsletters which you can search by keyword and subject. It also contains an archive of published material since January 1999. You can access a directory of barristers, law firms, law schools, partnership firms and recruitment consultants, and print out articles and other information from the site.

In the next chapter we present some sites related to the core law curriculum.

Miscellaneous research tools

Barrister-at-Law
http://www.barrister-at-law.org.uk/
This is a legal practice web site which offers free listings and summaries of key UK and European legal web sites. It deals with solicitors' practices, barristers' chambers and a wide range of resources from law books and CD-ROMs to legal periodicals.

Hieros Gamos
http://www.hg.org/
This is a substantial and well-presented US and international law portal, which can even be viewed in several different European languages.

LawCrawler
http://lawcrawler.lp.findlaw.com/
This is a law-centred search engine maintained by FindLaw and powered byAltaVista. It can be used to narrow searches to particular jurisdictions. You can search with Boolean operators such as AND, OR, NEAR, and NOT, and search for worldwide (not just US) web sites. This site is apt to produce as much non-legal as legal material.

Social Science Information Gateway
http://www.sosig.ac.uk/
SOSIG aims to provide a trusted source of selected, high quality Internet information for researchers and practitioners in the social sciences, business and law. It is part of the UK Resource Discovery

Researching on the internet..

Network. From the home page, follow the links to Law, Law By Subject Area, and UK Law.

Starting Points for Legal Research on the Internet
http://www.bris.ac.uk/Depts/Law/other.html#schuk
Developed at Bristol University, this page offers a set of jumping-off points for legal research on the web.

---

rks   Location: http://www.bris.ac.uk/Depts/Law/other.html#schuk   ▼ What's Rela

Miscellaneous sites, gateways and search engines

Legal Information Services
> This site is provided by the Law Technology Centre at the University of Warwick. (The LTC is the CTI (Computers in Teaching Initiative) centre for Law.) This site is also host to the National Centre for Legal Education and the Law Courseware Consortium.

Lawlinks
> Sarah Carter, the Law Librarian at the University of Kent, has produced a very comprehensive catalogue of links, covering the world of law.

Legal Resources Pages
> This site, maintained by Delia Venables, has links to legal websites, as well as computer and technology-related information for lawyers.

Information for Lawyers
> This company has a comprehensive site, which provides information for and about the UK legal community.

AustLII
> The Australasian Legal Information Institute is probably the best source of free legal information on the Internet. It offers hyperlinked judgments of Australian courts, as well as marked-up legislation.

Cornell Law School Legal Information Institute
> A comprehensive starting point for American legal research. This site is especially good for information on the US Supreme Court, including full-text judgments.

World Wide Web Virtual Library: Law
> Part of the WWW virtual library project, the oldest catalogue of the web. This site tends to be a little US-centric.

Social Science Information Gateway

University of Dundee Legal Web Sites Library
http://www.dundee.ac.uk/law/legal/index.htm
Here you will find a collection of law-related links intended for students, academics and professional lawyers. They are organised under such headings as charity law, civil liberties, criminal law, commercial law, English law, environmental law, European law, family law, gender law, immigration and nationality, IT law, intellectual property, law schools, legal academics, legal firms, legal publishers, law search sites, public and administrative law, public international law, socio-legal matters, sSots law, statutes and case reports, and UK resources.

More Internet Handbooks to help you

Law & Lawyers on the Internet, Stephen Hardy.
Where to Find It on the Internet, Kye Valongo (2nd edition)

4 The core legal curriculum

What is the core law curriculum? The phrase refers students to the subjects required to give them exemption from law professional exams. These subjects include: constitutional and administrative law (these days often known as public law); criminal law; European law; the law of obligations (contract/tort); human rights/civil liberties (including police powers); and property law (including equity/trusts and land law). The core subjects also include the English Legal System, or the Introduction to Law as it is more commonly known. This covers the sources of law, the courts system (both national and European), all matters considered in the preceding chapters of this book. Consequently, this chapter seeks to introduce some key sites for students in these 'core' areas:

▶ *constitutional and administrative law (public law)*
▶ *criminal law*
▶ *contract and tort law (law of obligation)*
▶ *European law*
▶ *human rights and civil liberties*
▶ *law of obligations*
▶ *property law*

Students should note that when using the net to search for sites on these core law topics they should beware of US sites and others proclaiming to state UK law. More important is this site:

http://www.omega23.com/Reference/k24k15-legal-clicks.html

which presents a continuously updated A-Z site of law. As its name suggests, it comes with 'quick clicks' presenting legal information in topic order. See also:

www.lawoffice.com

and the Jurist site, referred to earlier. Each of these provides answers to basic questions and access to relevant materials. These sites are particularly useful for all the core law subjects, supplying information on the basic principles and the latest books available.

Constitutional and administrative law (public law)

Constitutional and administrative law is part of the law often referred to as public law, but which regulates the relationship between the citizen and the state. Given this description you might argue that this law which is the body of government. Evidently, many of the government sites quoted above might be useful. However, the selected sites below provide some starting points for topics likely to be covered in coursework and/or assignment and examinations:

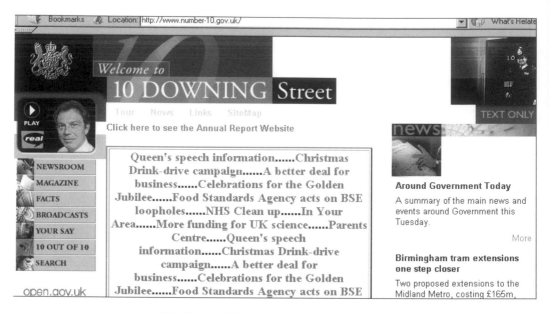

Fig. 23. The web site of the Prime Minister's Office at Number 10 Downing Street.

The Prime Minister.
http://www.number-10.gov.uk
This is the web site of the prime minister. It not only provides a virtual look inside this famous London address, but sets out government news and the PM's speeches. Regular features include:

1. a Newsroom – today's big stories in government and the latest response to issues in the news, plus speeches and interviews by the prime minister

2. a magazine – features on events and people around government, plus a virtual tour of the Downing Street building

3. facts – in-depth background on key policies, including delivery of the government's manifesto

4. broadcasts – by the prime minister from Downing Street and the House of Commons

5. Your Say – an interactive moderated discussion forum which lets you put your views direct to the government.

Parliament
http://www.parliament.uk
This site covers how the British Parliament works and covers both Houses – the Commons and the Lords. It publishes daily lists and Hansard reports. The links include Explore Parliament (a parliamentary web site for schools), further information about Parliamentary services, a guide to the Parliamentary system, visits, a bookshop,

and archives. In this modern age of devolution, see also the following web sites:

Northern Ireland Assembly
http://www.ni-assembly.gov.uk

Scottish Parliament
http://www.scottish.parliament.uk/
The pages of this site cover all the essential information about the Parliament, its members and proceedings. You can look at MSP biographies online, and even find MSPs by postcode.

Welsh Assembly
http://www.wales.gov.uk/index_e.html
This is the Welsh Assembly's web page (English version). Again it covers its membership and proceedings. Note the bilingual nature of the web site, and its accessibility.

Although students of 'con and admin' law might be asked questions about the office of PM, the powers of Parliament – especially its supremacy, and the question of devolution – it is also likely that questions about the monarchy will be set. To answer such questions see:

The Monarchy
http://www.royal.gov.uk
This site presents the monarchy – the House of Windsor – with information, diary pages, an internet visitor's book and some very useful historical pages. It makes an excellent reference point for questions on the Royal Prerogative.

Fig. 24. The British monarchy web site. Follow the links to Your Questions Answered

The core legal curriculum ....

In terms of Parliamentary reform the Parliament site above gives some information, but it also contains a link site to the Royal Commission on House of Lords Reform.

Furthermore, as students will be aware, since constitutional and administrative law – in particular the administrative element – covers judicial review and remedies, then the High Court site given above will also be of value. In addition, the sites of tribunals, accessed through the LCD's site, will provide other useful information, as will the ombudsman site, accessed by the same means.

Criminal law

Criminal law covers offences against the State for wrongdoing. As Smith and Hogan, the long-standing and leading academics in the field suggest: 'An attempt to define a crime at once encounters a serious difficulty.' Once students have grappled with the central terms mens rea and actus reus, they soon understand what the confusion is all about.

Criminal law remains complex since it relies on human actions and motives, and then defences, and the proper functioning of courts as well as other bodies of various kinds. Beneath this plethora of concepts are the further complications of procedures, powers and controversial offences – theft, assault, homicide, sexual, property, public order, incitement, conspiracy and attempt. Whilst the web sites reviewed below do not cover these huge topics directly, they do provide information on where you can find the latest criminal law articles and the institutions which cover criminal law.

British Journal of Criminology
http://www.oup.co.uk/crimin/
The British Journal of Criminology site provides students with access to articles and news on current developments in criminal law. The site is maintained by the Oxford University Press.

Criminal Law Review
http://elj.warwick.ac.uk/juk/journals/clr1.html
The site, hosted by the University of Warwick, gives information and access to the Criminal Law Review, the acclaimed journal for criminal law.

Criminal Law Links
http://snipe.ukc.ac.uk/law/spu/crimjust.htm
This criminal law links site, provided by the University of Kent, offers students access to statutes, case law, journals and other commentaries on criminal law.

Institutions of the criminal law

Crown Prosecution Service
http://www.cps.gov.uk/cps$$home.htm
The CPS is the government department which prosecutes people in England and Wales who have been charged by the police with a criminal offence. The CPS was created by the Prosecution of Offences Act 1985. It is independent of the police, although it works closely with them. Within each of its 42 local areas are one or more branch offices handling local prosecutions and headed by a Branch Crown Prosecutor. In 1997-98, the branches dealt with 1.4 million cases in the Magistrates' Courts and 128,064 in the Crown Courts. The site provides information on sentencing. The site includes a Welsh language version. This is a good resource for essays concerned with the enforcement of criminal law.

Lord Chancellor's Department: Criminal Matters
http://www.open.gov.uk/lcd/criminal/crimfr.htm
This site gives details of guidance, policy initiatives and recent case law and statutes affecting criminal law. This site provides the latest information from the Lord Chief Justice.

European Court of Human Rights
http://www.dhcour.coe.fr/
The European Court of Human Rights site, as noted above, gives information on enforcing and interpreting the rights of citizens held under the 1950 European Convention on Human Rights. This has become more important to criminal practitioners since 2 November 2000 with the enactment and coming into force of the 1998 Human Rights Act. This site will be of immense value in this regard.

Fig. 25. The European Court of Human Rights. Find out here about pending cases, and the latest judgments and decisions.

Criminal Cases Review Commission
http://www.ccrc.gov.uk
The Criminal Cases Review Commission independently investigates any alleged miscarriages of Justice. Its site provides guidance and forms on how to complain.

Home Office
http://www.homeoffice.gov.uk
As students should be aware from constitutional and administrative law, the Home Office is the government department responsible for internal affairs in England and Wales. Its main business is law and order. The home page has links to constitutional and community issues, human rights, race equality, freedom of information, data protection, elections, political parties and European issues; crime reduction, the latest crime figures, criminal justice, prisons, the police, probation and courts, the emergency services, disaster management, immigration, passports and lots more.

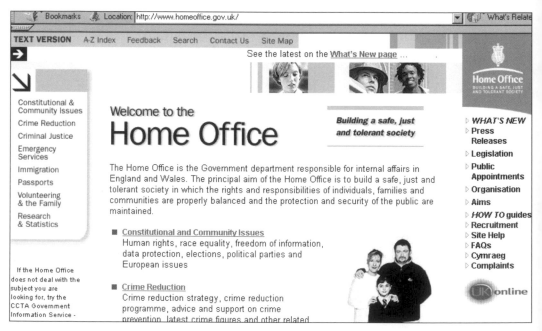

Fig. 26. The Home Office has a substantial web site of value to students. If the Home Office does not deal with the subject you are looking for, you can also try the CCTA Govt Information Service (www.open.gov.uk) which links to other government web sites.

Law Commission
http://www.gtnet.gov.uk/lawcomm/
The Law Commission is the statutory law reform body in the UK. Its site gives information on the latest Law Reform proposals. Useful information for students on 'corporate manslaughter' is given here.

Prison Service
http://www.hmprisonservice.gov.uk/
Her Majesty's Prison Service serves the public by keeping in custody

those committed by the courts, and organises and administers the British prison system. Its web site apparently attracts around 34,000 hits per month. There is a link to Her Majesty's Chief Inspector of Prisons for England and Wales.

Youth Justice Board
http://www.youth-justice-board.gov.uk
The Youth Justice Board for England and Wales, is a new executive non-departmental public body established on 30 September 1998 under the Crime and Disorder Act 1998, to advise on the supervision and administration of youth justice within England and Wales.

Prisons Handbook
http://www.tphbook.dircon.co.uk/
This site offers an online Prisons Handbook, a definitive annual guide to the penal system of England and Wales. It has become established as the principal source of reference for the penal system of England and Wales since the first edition appeared in 1995. In 1996 the Prison Service instructed the governors of all prisons and young offender institutions in England and Wales to stock it in both their inmate and staff libraries. It is also a required text on many law and criminology courses.

European Law

According to the Treaty of Amsterdam 1998: 'The EU marks the process of creating an ever closer union among the peoples of Europe... who seek to promote economic and social progress...'. European law governs this Union of European peoples. To that end, European law is supreme (see the cases of *Costa v. Enel*, *Simmenthal*, *and Van Gend*). Students of law therefore cannot escape the impact and influence of Europe on our domestic legal system.

The sites described below give access to the sources of European law, in order to assist students in addressing such questions as: the European New legal order, European legal supremacy, the EU institutions, the free movement of goods, capital, workers and services, equal treatment, and competition law. In addition, European law, albeit not covered by the Treaty of Rome (as amended) also covers human rights law, derived from the 1950 European Convention on Human Rights.

Europa
http://europa.eu.int/index-en.htm
As noted above in Chapters 2 and 3, the ECJ can be accessed using this site and its case law traced and downloaded. See also:

europa.eu.int/cj/en/index.htm

European Court of Human rights in Strasbourg
http://www.dhcour.coe.fr/default.htm
This page marks the home of the European Court of Human rights in Strasbourg and guardian and interpreter of the 1950 European Convention on Human Rights. The web site as a whole gives you access to case law, legislation, opinions, a short history of the Court, and an explanation of its function.

University of Hull
http://www.hull.ac.uk/php/lbsebd/eia$$html/access1.htm
The University of Hull acts as the link-way to the European Information Association's site, giving students up-to-date news from the EU institutions on all matters of policy.

European Law Office
http://www.europeanlawoffice.com
The European Law Office is a very useful site, providing access to legal news as it emerges, as well as commentaries on current EU law.

Fig. 27. The European Law Office offers a wide range of newsletters, covering everything from arbitration to white collar crime. The site is an online service of Globe Business Publishing Ltd.

Law Firms in Europe
http://www.european-law-firm.com/links.htm
This hyperlink site gives access to law firms in Europe which specialise in European law. Some of these firms have updating services on their sites and offer case law commentaries. Sometimes these can give students insights into the mechanics of EU law.

Institute for European Law
http://www.iel.bham.ac.uk/
Hosted by the University of Birmingham, the Institute for European Law provides many useful links to other European law sites. Students are recommended to use this site to access wider information.

Human rights and civil liberties

This core subject is a mix of old and new. In former times, the phrase 'civil liberties' covered UK police powers. British law students were taught that since the UK had an unwritten constitution, its subjects had limited rights.

Today human rights law, to some extent the successor to civil liberties, has established that UK citizens do have rights – as European citizens. Consult your passport for further details and note that British subjects have held EU passports since 1 November 1993. This debate may end after 2 November 2000 and the full incorporation of the 1950 European Convention on Human Rights into law under the 1998 Human Rights Act. The web sites below illustrate some useful sources and issues in this debate:

1 Crown Office Row
http://www.onecrownofficerow.com/hru/index.htm
This chambers' site from 1 Crown Office Row includes specialist barristers in immigration law. It gives a Human Rights Act 1998 update. It also discusses and offers services on the Human Rights Act, Human Rights Convention and Strasbourg law – legal documents of fundamental importance to lawyers preparing cases when the Act comes into force.

Electronic Immigration Network
http://www.ein.org.uk
The Electronic Immigration Network is a charity relating to immigration, refugee and nationality law and practice in the UK. It presents a site containing a comprehensive list of links to other sites related to immigration and human rights issues, both in this country and around the world (take 'Resources'). A subscription service offers access to all Immigration Appeal Tribunal determinations and relevant reports from higher courts.

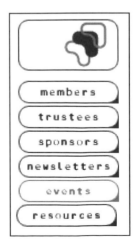

Human Rights Web
http://www.hrweb.org
The Human Rights Web offers a comprehensive service of advice, information and references on immigration and human rights law. This is a very useful site for law students.

Immigration Advisory Service
http://www.vois.org.uk/ias/
The Immigration Advisory Service describes itself as the largest and

Bookmarks   **Location:** http://www.hrweb.org/   ▼ 🗔 Wh

What are Human Rights?

- An Introduction to Human Rights
- A Short History of the Human Rights Movement
- Biographies of Prisoners of Conscience

Human Rights Legal and Political Documents

- United Nations Documents
- Other Documents
- Human Rights Issues, Debates, and Discussions

What can I do to Promote Human Rights?

- Getting Started: A Primer for New Human Rights Activists
- Join a Human Rights Organization!

Human Rights Resources

Human Rights Web Administrative Page

Fig. 28. The Human Rights Web. There is a very useful link to a large number of online human rights resources.

most experienced charity giving free advice and representation in immigration and asylum matters. It has regional offices in Birmingham, Cardiff, Central London, Gatwick, Glasgow, Hounslow, Leeds and Manchester. The IAS deals with over 7,500 appeals and 20,000 telephone enquiries every year.

Immigration Law Practitioners' Association
http://www.ein.org.uk/ilpa/
The Immigration Law Practitioners' Association (better known as ILPA) is the UK's professional association of lawyers and academics practising in or concerned about immigration, asylum and nationality law. Its membership currently stands at 650. Membership is by application supported by two references and subject to an annual membership fee. It is only open to persons subject to a professional disciplinary body. Immigration Law relating to English speaking countries is provided by BCL Immigration Services. There is also a collection of privacy and encryption material.

Legal Action Group
http://www.lag.org.uk
Law students over the last two decades have become acquainted with the Legal Action Group. LAG is the national, independent charity which campaigns for equal access to justice for all members of society. It provides support to lawyers and advisers, inspires developments in that practice, and campaigns for improvements in the law.

National Association of Citizens Advice Bureaux
http://www.nacab.org.uk/
Local Citizens Advice Bureaux (CABs) and their national sister organisation, the National Association of Citizens Advice Bureaux (NACAB), offer a wide-range of information and statistical research on today's salient social issues, for example poverty, exclusion, money advice, debts, housing and social security benefits.

RightsNet
http://www.rightsnet.org.uk
This site presents the RightsNet Discussion Forum. Students are recommended to give this try and join in the online debate.

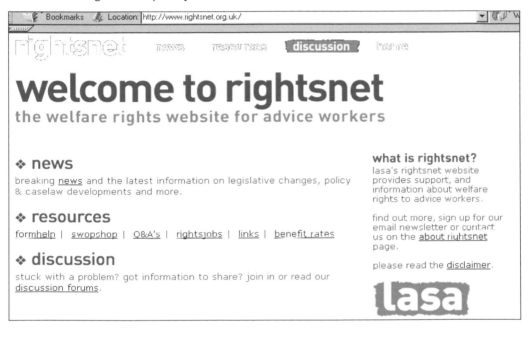

Law of obligations (contract, tort)

The modern law of obligations encapsulates two well-established areas of law:

1. tort – civil wrong, liability and negligence, etc

2. contract – the law on agreements and bargaining.

Clearly, these two legal areas regulate much of our everyday lives, for example. Buying goods in shops, crossing the road, sales and goods, product liabilitythe list is almost endless. Negligence, misstatement, consideration and duress are just a few of the topics to be covered in this wide-ranging area. Below are some web sites which will help students to get started:

Fig. 29. The Rights Net discussion forums debate such topics as incapacity and disability, jobseekers and the New Deal scheme, family benefits, people coming from abroad, young people and students, and new legislation and case law.

The core legal curriculum..

Butterworths
http://www.butterworths.com
This site of Butterworths Publishers gives details of the Journal of Contract Law and other Tort texts.

Contractual Issues
http://www.visionautics.com/depaul/classnotes/Inter~1/sld056.htm
This site covers the contractual issues of duties, terms, custom and practice, warranties, disclaimers, unconscionability and privity.

Economic Contract Law
http://www.visionautics.com/depaul/classnotes/Intera~1/sld056.htm
This site introduces Economic Contract Law. It should be very useful to students struggling with the concept of how law and economics merge.

Law Professor
http://spinoza.tau.ac.il/humor/lw/lw_23.htm
A law professor answers your contractual questions – an interesting site to explore.

Law Students
http://www.lawstudents.org/contracts/outline/html
This site provides a basic outline of the law of contract.

Tort Law Message Board
http://www.lawstudents.org/wwwboard7/wwboard.html
The Tort Law Message Board presents the issues and/or of the day in the Law of Tort. It makes a very useful noticeboard for students.

▶ *Note* – As law students will be aware, since the 1996 Civil Justice Reforms, under the directorship of the Master of the Rolls, Lord Woolf, contract law has undergone some changes, summarised below. These changes have impacted immensely upon the procedural nature of the law of obligations.

UK Government Information Service: Civil Justice Reform
http://www.open.gov.uk/lcd/civil/inter.htm
This site presents the UK Government Information Service's Civil Justice Reform: Interim Report.

The Woolf Report
http://www.open.gov.uk/lcd/civil/interim/woolf.htm
This is a web site for the Woolf Report, more commonly known as Access To Justice, authored by The Right Honourable the Lord Woolf, July 1996. This sets out the detailed Woolf Reforms which affect civil litigation.

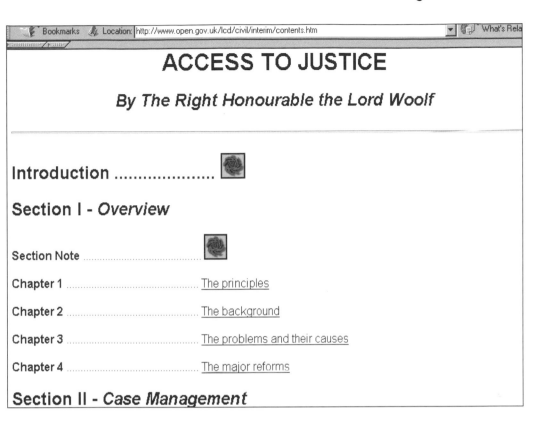

Fig. 30. The Woolf Report. The web site includes the text plus a useful summary of its main 124 recommendations.

Civil Justice Reform
http://www.open.gov.uk/lcd/civil/progrfr.htm
This site considers the implementation of the Civil Justice Reform and gives updated progress reports,

The growth in civil litigation has developed the area of consumer law, especially product liability. The web sites described below are those of the related enforcement agencies.

Consumer Gateway
http://www.consumer.gov.uk
The Consumer Gateway provides advice, government reports, and information on cars, finance, food, home improvement and utilities. It also explains on to complain and to which bodies.

Office of Fair Trading
http://www.oft.gov.uk
The Office of Fair Trading site provides not only commentaries on relevant law and legal developments, but information on how to take action under civil law. There are also links to various consumer advice groups.

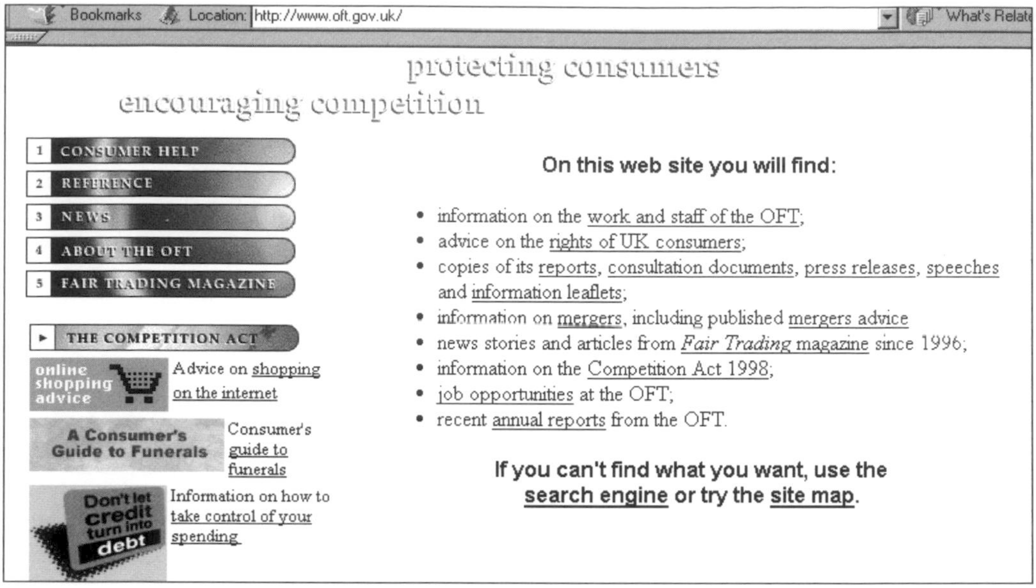
Bookmarks
Location: http://www.oft.gov.uk/
What's Related
protecting consumers
encouraging competition
1 CONSUMER HELP
2 REFERENCE
3 NEWS
4 ABOUT THE OFT
5 FAIR TRADING MAGAZINE
THE COMPETITION ACT
online shopping advice
Advice on shopping on the internet
A Consumer's Guide to Funerals
Consumer's guide to funerals
Don't let credit turn into debt
Information on how to take control of your spending
On this web site you will find:
information on the work and staff of the OFT;
advice on the rights of UK consumers;
copies of its reports, consultation documents, press releases, speeches and information leaflets;
information on mergers, including published mergers advice
news stories and articles from Fair Trading magazine since 1996;
information on the Competition Act 1998;
job opportunities at the OFT;
recent annual reports from the OFT.
If you can't find what you want, use the search engine or try the site map.

Fig. 31. The web site of the Office of Fair Trading (OFT).

Trading Standards Net
http://www.xodesign.co.uk/tsnet/
The Trading Standards Net gives information on the general role of Trading Standards, where and how to contact them, and how they can help complainants.

Students of the law of obligations will rapidly become acquainted with a Paisley snail and an alleged cure for influenza (see Donoghue v. Stevenson, and Carlill v. Carbolic Smoke Ball Co.).

Property law

Property law covers a wealth of specialist areas, including land law, landlord and tenant, housing, trusts and the law of equity and probate (wills). To that end, students should be aware of the many sites dealing with intellectual property (on specialist copyright law) which should be avoided for the time being.

Furthermore, students should read documents carefully to ensure that they cover English law. Many property law web sites cover Canadian, United States and Australian law. These have some similarities with English law, but many distinguishing features, too.

EGi Property Law Service
http://www.propertylaw.co.uk
EGi Property Law Service provides updates on case law and regulations, and other legal developments. The site is a project of the leading weekly property magazine, Estates Gazette.

HM Land Registry
http://www.open.gov.uk/landreg/home.htm
This is the HM Land Registry web site. It can be used for performing registration, gaining information and conducting searches.

FindLaw
http://www.findlaw.com/01topics/33property/index.html
This web page offers access to sites containing cases on property law.

Trusts and Trustees
http://www.trusts-and-trustees.com/
This site introduces the concept of trusts and trustees, presenting articles to do with all aspects of trusts.

A Crash Course in Wills and Trusts
http://www.mtpalermo.com/
This site is best described as a 'crash course in wills and trusts'. It also provides the information you need for estate planning and related matters such as probate, gifts, and estate tax. It gives some good examples for students of trusts and the various types.

Estate Web
http://www.estateweb.com/common/trusts.htm
This site offers students another source for information about trusts and wills.

Fig. 32. The EGi Property Law Service. It is run by Estates Gazette, the leading weekly journal for property professionals.

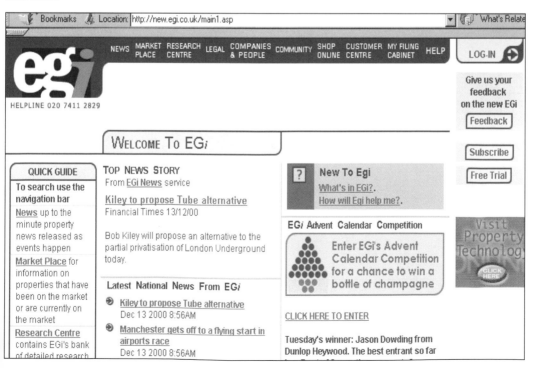

Landlord and Tenant Law
http://www.surveying.salford.ac.uk/course/law/property%20.
Law.htm
This is a useful and simple to understand guide to landlord and tenant law.

▶ *Recommended sources* – Students should remember when re-searching the Core Law areas to seek advice from their tutors, both as to useful web sites and recommended texts. Also, your own law school may have posted its own web pages containing course information, module specifications and of course, useful course notes and other helpful resources.

In the next chapter we provide short reviews of informational web sites dealing with the British legal profession.

5 The UK legal profession

This chapter examines the British legal professions and their associations. Since the UK legal profession is divided into two – solicitors and barristers, or advocates for the latter in Scotland – this chapter is divided in the same manner, providing information on their training, governing bodies and networking contacts:

▶ *barristers and advocates*
▶ *solicitors*
▶ *professional associations*

. . . .

Barristers and advocates

Today there are some 14,000 barristers in England, and around 6,000 advocates in Scotland. Barristers practise in chambers and are governed by the Bar Council.

The Bar Council
http://www.barcouncil.org.uk
Based in Bedford Row, London, the Bar Council is the governing body of English barristers. Its web site covers the origins, history and role of the Bar and includes current contact information, press releases and information about its various activities. The Council deals with the qualification and conduct rules governing barristers and those wishing to become barristers. It deals with complaints against

Fig. 33. The Bar Council. The About Barristers pages provide useful historical information about barristers and descriptions of what they do. The Rules and Guidance pages contain the rules and guidance affecting barristers including the Code of Conduct.

The Bar Council

The General Council of the Bar®

Click here to enter the website...

Main Offices:
3 Bedford Row, London WC1R 4DB Tel: 020 7242 0082
Complaints Department:
Northumberland House, 3rd Floor 303 - 306 High Holborn, London, WC1V 7JZ Tel: 020 7440 4000
Education & Training & Video Conferencing:
2/3 Cursitor Street, London EC4A 1NE Tel: 020 7440 4000

barristers. They say: 'It also puts the Bar's view on matters of concern about the legal system and acts as a source of information about the Bar. This site contains information for a diverse audience: if you are a barrister; a solicitor looking to instruct a barrister; looking to qualify as a barrister; or a member of the public, there is information here for you.'

Butterworth
http://www.butterworths.co.uk/bld
Similarly, the Butterworth's Legal Directory is an online version of the print publication. This is a directory of solicitors and barristers in private practice, commerce, local government and public authorities in England, Northern Ireland, Scotland and Wales. The database is searchable by organisation or by individual.

Inns of Court
http://www.online-law.co.uk/bar/inns_of_court.html
The four Inns of Court are described here. You will find some interesting historical background about each, and links to some of the chambers in each.

LINCOLN'S INN

Kennedy Guide to Barristers & Expert Witnesses
http://www.kennedyguidebarristers.com/
This is a directory of barristers in the United Kingdom. The site says: 'This is the first internet directory of its kind that allows barristers to update their entries themselves, as and when changes occur. It also includes attributed endorsements from solicitors. These features help ensure that the user of the guide has the most current information in order to make a more informed choice of counsel.'

Solicitors

INNER TEMPLE

Presently, there are more than 70,000 solicitors in the UK. Established as a profession in 1605, solicitors make up the largest of the two branches of the UK legal profession. They have been governed by the Law Society since 1843, and are now governed under the 1974 Solicitors Act. Solicitors are often described as the 'general practitioners of law'.

Law Society
http://www.lawsociety.org.uk
Whether you are a solicitor, a citizen, in business, a law student, a trainee, working in a law practice, or just browsing, you will find lots o useful information here. The Law Society is the regulatory body for Solicitors in England and Wales. The web site provides information on solicitors, career opportunities, policy notes, and law links. You will also find the latest edition of the Law Society Gazette online and you can search its recruitment ads. There are links to: who we are, legal education, recruitment, directory of solicitors, professional training

and accreditation, members services, law and policy, the Law Society Gazette, and the office for the supervision of solicitors.

Law Society of Ireland

http://www.lawsociety.ie/

The Law Society is the educational, representative and regulatory body of the solicitors' profession in Ireland. It was established in 1773 and now exercises statutory functions under the Solicitors Acts 1954-1994 in relation to the education, admission, enrolment, discipline and regulation of the profession. It works to improve access to the law generally and also provides representation, services and support for solicitors themselves. The Society also deals with complaints from the public about members of the profession and administers a statutory compensation fund. There are currently over 5,000 solicitors practising in Ireland. The web site provides an overview of the work of the solicitors' profession and of The Law Society in Ireland. There are links to education with details on becoming an apprentice and qualifying as a solicitor in Ireland; the Gazette, the journal of the Law Society; and links to useful internet sites of interest to legal practitioners.

Law Society of Scotland

http://www.lawscot.org.uk

The Law Society of Scotland is the governing body of the solicitor branch of the Scottish legal profession. All practising solicitors in Scotland must be members and take out a practising certificate. The Society has a Council of 50 members, 42 elected by constituents of

Fig. 34. The Law Society of Scotland web site includes Dial-a-Law, an information and referral service with a library of over 40 different legal topics ranging from family law to employment law.

areas they represent and 8 co-opted from industry, commerce, and central and local government. Council elects annually a President and Vice President. The Society has committees monitoring and developing services in legal education, law reform, professional practice and ethics, complaints handling, professional remuneration, professional indemnity, legal aid, property marketing, international relations, and marketing and public relations.

new search

search results

about this site

the law society

a-z index

about solicitors

specialist panels

using solicitors

Solicitors Online
http://www.solicitors-online.com/
This is a searchable listing of solicitors and firms regulated by the Law Society records. It includes all solicitors who work in private practice law firms and who also have a current practising certificate issued by the Law Society of England and Wales. You can search by name or by specialism – ADR/mediation, civil litigation, commercial and company law, conveyancing, criminal law, EU law, family law, human rights law, and legal aid. The site includes information on qualifying as a solicitor.

Legal Resources in the UK and Ireland
http://www.venables.co.uk/
This excellent and substantial site, maintained by Delia Venables, provides information on firms of solicitors worldwide, including UK law firms.

Professional associations

Below are some of the main sites for students to view in relation to professional law associations.

Alliance for Interactive Media Law
http://www.alliancelaw.com/
This is an alliance of United States and European law firms which provide state of the art legal services to the interactive and multimedia industry

Association of Child Abuse Lawyers
http://www.abny.demon.co.uk/acal/
The Association and its web site offer practical support for lawyers and other professionals working for adults and children who have been abused. The site gives details of training courses, and a newsletter.

Association of Commercial Lawyers International
http://www.acl-int.com
The ACL is a network of 38 firms comprising over 800 lawyers. Member firms around the world offer advice and a global service to clients. The ACL offers clients the benefits of local representation in a foreign jurisdiction and local knowledge of cross-border transactions.

Association of Conditional Fee Lawyers
http://www.acfl.co.uk
The Association of Conditional Fee Lawyers has been founded to represent the interests of those lawyers who act, or will be acting, in the field of 'no win, no fee'. It has initially been founded to represent the interests of solicitors and may extend to represent the interests of barristers, experts and clients as well.

Association of Independent European Lawyers
http://www.aiel.com/
Formed in 1991, in anticipation of the European Open Market, the aim of the Association is to provide a network of independent English speaking legal firms, throughout the European Union, which can refer and interact on behalf of commercial clients across the various legal systems.

Association of Law Teachers
http://www.smlawpub.co.uk/academic/alt/About.htm
For membership information see the link to subscriptions. The Association publishes the journal Law Teacher.

Association of Lawyers & Legal Advisors
http://www.lawyers-assoc.com
The Association of Lawyers & Legal Advisors, the Lawyers' Movement, was founded in 1995 as an organisation of lawyers, legal advisors and legal service providers operating in a specialised area of law. The main purpose of the Association is to accredit members by way of a grading system.

Association of Lawyers for Children
http://www.alc.org.uk
The Association evolved from an idea put forward at the first annual conference organised by child care solicitors and was inaugurated at the third National Conference in Manchester in 1992. Membership includes those lawyers involved in work relating to children – solicitors, barristers and legal staff. The Association also offers associate membership to others involved in working with or for children such as psychiatrists, psychologists, social workers, paediatricians and guardians.

Association of Pension Lawyers
http://www.apl.org.uk/
The APL is for lawyers specialising in pensions in the UK. It aims to promote awareness of the importance of the role of pensions law and to operate as a forum for discussion and education amongst pension lawyers. Its members are individuals, not organisations. On this web site, you will find details of who is eligible for membership and application forms if you wish to join. You will also find information about

various publications, conferences and training programmes, a diary of events, details of members of the Association's committees and local groups and more.

APIL members

what's new

APIL diary

press and parliamentary

benefits of membership

Association of Personal Injury Lawyers
http://www.apil.com/
APIL is dedicated to improving the service provided to victims of accident and clinical negligence. More than 4,500 solicitors and barristers work with the Association to fight for law reform to improve access to justice.

British and Irish Legal Education Technology Association
http://www.bileta.ac.uk
BILETA was formed in 1986 with the primary objective of promoting technology in legal education throughout the United Kingdom and Ireland. It works in conjunction with the UK Centre for Legal Education.

British Legal Association
http://www.britishlegal.org.uk/
The BLA is an association of solicitors, trainee solicitors and barristers drawn from all parts of England and Wales. It was originally formed in 1964 as a protest against Law Society leadership at the time. It publishes a journal, Independent Solicitor.

Discrimination Law Association
http://www.parish.oaktree.co.uk/dla/dla1.htm

about us

join ela

press

members

elakol

Employment Lawyers Association
http://www.elaweb.org.uk/
Since its inception in 1992 the ELA has become an authoritative voice on employment law. Its members are qualified lawyers, both barristers and solicitors, practising in employment law in the UK, and organisations engaged in the practice of employment law.

Euro-American Lawyers Group
http://www.ealg.com
This is an international association of law firms in the US and Europe. Since its inception in 1985 EALG has steadily developed, and now comprises 365 lawyers working in 21 different jurisdictions.

Eurojuris International
http://www.eurojuris.net/
Eurojuris International is a grouping of over 700 law firms in 18 countries throughout Europe and Scandinavia, and covering 650 different cities/locations. The group is composed of 18 national Eurojuris Associations, bringing together medium-sized law firms from each particular country.

Fig. 35. Eurojuris aims to help business enterprises and individuals facing legal and judicial problems in a 'Europe without borders'.

Euro-Link for Lawyers

http://www.eurolink-law.com

As the title to this site suggests, it offers a Euro link for lawyers It is one of the largest international legal networks and legal associations in the world. It acts as a facilitator of international legal services bringing together the combined strengths of over 50 commercial legal practices and law firms, with more than 425 partners and 65 offices worldwide.

Fig. 36. Headquartered in Switzerland, Eurolink is a network of European law firms. It publishes News Link, a business newsletter.

European Law Firms

http://www.european-law-firm.com

This is a grouping of EU law firms and non-EU associate members offering legal services throughout the European Union, and across its internal and external frontiers. It brings together some 250 lawyers practising in all areas of business law.

Forum of Insurance Lawyers

http://www.foil.org.uk

FOIL exists to provide a forum for the exchange of information between lawyers acting predominantly or exclusively for insurance clients, either practising within firms of solicitors, as barristers or as in-house lawyers for insurers or for self-insurers.

Freelance Solicitors Group

http://members.aol.com/pjmiller00/freelance.html

The Freelance Solicitors Group was originally founded in September 1993 as the Locum Solicitors Group. It represents the interests of those solicitors in England and Wales who work as solicitor for others on a locum, contract or freelance basis. The Group maintains a locum list, and organises various social events.

Immigration Law Practitioners Association

http://www.ilpa.org.uk/

ILPA was established in 1984 by a group of leading UK immigration practitioners to promote and improve the advising and representation of immigrants; to provide information to members on domestic and European immigration, refugee and nationality law; and to secure a non-racist, non-sexist, just and equitable system of immigration, refugee and nationality law. ILPA has around 900 members including lawyers, advice workers, academics and law students.

International Law Association

http://www.ila-hq.org

The ILA site gives information on International resolutions and treaties from the headquarters of this international non-governmental organisation. The Association's history dates back to 1873 and many of its past and present Officers are leaders in the field of international law.

International Legal Group

http://www.intlegalgroup.com

This is a worldwide network of independent law firms. They provide a 'search service for individuals and globalising companies to locate high quality law firms that match their specific needs worldwide. An energy company will have a different legal need than a high-tech software company, and an individual with an estate problem in Brazil, Pakistan or elsewhere will need a totally different law firm –

so we look for the right match in each case if we don't already have a member with those skills in the country specified.'

International Network of Independent Lawyers
http://www.advoc.com
The web site provides access to legal services across frontiers, throughout Europe, Asia and the Middle East.

Jurist: The Legal Education Network
http://www.law.cam.ac.uk/jurist/index.htm
This is a very useful legal education network hosted by the University of Cambridge Faculty of Law. The web site covers UK law schools, prospectuses, staff, and libraries; law school news with clippings and reports on legal education; resources for UK law teachers; and tips for law students and more.

Justices' Clerk's Society
http://www.jc-society.co.uk
The Society was founded in 1839 and incorporated in 1903. It is a professional body representing the principal legal advisers to lay magistrates in England and Wales and is committed to improving the quality of justice in magistrates' courts. One of its main objects is to review the operation of the law, especially that administered by magistrates' courts in England and Wales, to point out its defects and to encourage proposals for improvement.

Fig. 37. The Justices Clerks Society aims to maintain the traditional role of the Justices' Clerk as personal adviser to a bench of magistrates, together with the role as senior administrator of the court or courts in which his magistrates sit.

The UK legal profession ....

Fig. 38. The Institute of Legal Executives web site includes information about syllabuses, qualifications, the CPD, law reform, colleges and more.

Institute of Legal Executives
http://www.ilex.org.uk

ILEX is the UK professional body representing over 22,000 legal executives and trainee legal executives. It promotes the profession of legal executive to career advisers, school leavers, graduates, mature students and those contemplating a change of career. Its web site has links to qualification route, the ILEX syllabus, questions answered, study options, and options and opportunities. The site also includes lists of colleges and local branches.

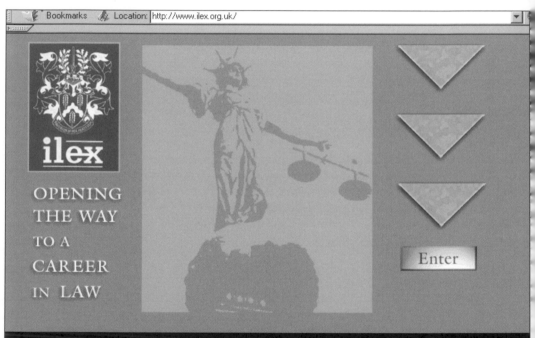

Law Centre Federation
http://www.lawcentres.org.uk

The Federation encourages the development of publicly funded legal services for those most disadvantaged in society and promotes the Law Centre model as the best means of achieving this. Centres offer free and independent professional legal advice to local people. The site lists the addresses of local offices and contains links to many organisations concerned with issues such as benefits, equal opportunities, health and housing, disability, and immigration.

Legal Action Group
http://www.lag.org.uk

LAG is a national independent charity which campaigns for equal access to justice for all members of society. It provides support to the practice of lawyers and advisers; inspires developments in that

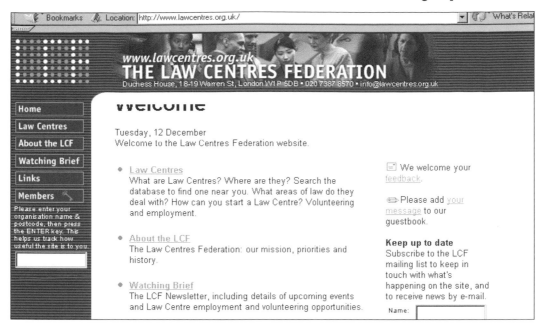

Bookmarks   Location: http://www.lawcentres.org.uk/   What's Rela

www.lawcentres.org.uk
THE LAW CENTRES FEDERATION
Duchess House, 18-19 Warren St, London W1P 5DB • 020 7387 8570 • info@lawcentres.org.uk

Home	**Welcome**
Law Centres	
About the LCF	Tuesday, 12 December
Watching Brief	Welcome to the Law Centres Federation website.
Links	
Members	• Law Centres

Please enter your organisation name & postcode; then press the ENTER key. This helps us track how useful the site is to you.

• **Law Centres**
What are Law Centres? Where are they? Search the database to find one near you. What areas of law do they deal with? How can you start a Law Centre? Volunteering and employment.

• **About the LCF**
The Law Centres Federation: our mission, priorities and history.

• **Watching Brief**
The LCF Newsletter, including details of upcoming events and Law Centre employment and volunteering opportunities.

We welcome your feedback.

Please add your message to our guestbook.

Keep up to date
Subscribe to the LCF mailing list to keep in touch with what's happening on the site, and to receive news by e-mail.

Name:

practice; campaigns for improvements in the law and the administration of justice; and stimulates debate on how services should be delivered.

Magistrates Association
http://www.magistrates-association.org.uk/
This is the web site of the Magistrates' Association, founded in 1920.

Medico-Legal Society
http://www.medico-legalsociety.org.uk
Founded in 1901, the Society aims to promote medico-legal knowledge in all its aspects. Its official organ is the Medico-Legal Journal.

Motor Accident Solicitors Society
http://www.mass.org.uk
MASS is an association of solicitors' firms, all with experience and expertise in the handling of motor accident claims. Member firms are located throughout the UK.

National Association of Paralegals
http://ourworld.compuserve.com/homepages/napl/
The Association offers a careers and qualifications route for those who for one reason or another do not qualify as a solicitor or a barrister in the UK. The main qualification is its Associate Qualification (Advanced Award in Paralegal Studies), which is run on an evening course basis by colleges throughout the UK.

Fig. 39. The Law Centres Federation. An online newsletter called Watching Brief provides details of upcoming events, together with Law Centre employment and volunteering opportunities.

Fig. 40. The Society for Computers and Law has set up some ecommerce working groups to examine controversial topics such as contract law electronically, electronic signatures, and security and workplace privacy.

Society for Computers and Law
http://www.scl.org/
The SCL exists to encourage and develop both information technology for lawyers and IT-related law. The web site contains details of its local branches, working groups, publications and more. Its membership now exceeds 2,000 and encompasses everyone from members of he judiciary to lawyers, teachers and IT managers.

Society of Public Teachers of Law
http://www.law.warwick.ac.uk/sptl/
The SPTL is the learned society of university lecturers. Founded in 1908, it gathers law academics together (your tutors do have friends, after all!). It aims to advance legal education, which includes teaching in universities, legal research and the professional training of lawyers. It organises a programme of seminars and has about twenty subject sections for members with particular legal interests.

Sole Practitioners Group
http://www.spg.uk.com
This is web site about solicitors who practise on their own account without partners. They may or may not employ other solicitor staff. Most of them have their own firms serving clients on a personal basis. There are about 4,800 sole practitioner solicitors in England and Wales.

Solicitors Family Law Association
http://www.sfla.org.uk
SFLA is an association of over 5,000 solicitors, started in 1982, whose members believe that aggressive lawyers and reliance on the court process can add to distress and anger on the breakdown of a family relationship. SFLA members abide by a code of practice designed to promote a conciliatory atmosphere in which matters are dealt with in a sensitive, constructive and cost-effective way.

UK Environmental Law Association
http://www.greenchannel.com/ukela/
The Association is not only open to lawyers. Many of its 1,000 or so members are scientists and others involved with environmental law, both in the UK and overseas.

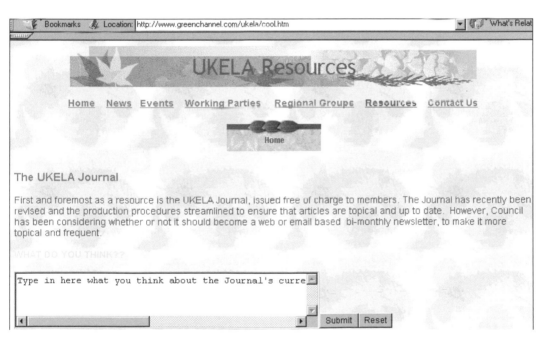

6 Law links for students

This chapter seeks to review salient legal sites for law students. Its aim is to ensure that students can key into important general student sites, as well as law specific ones. Below is a mixture of both. In this chapter we provide sites on:

▶ *legal education and training*
▶ *careers*
▶ *law libraries*
▶ *student law societies*
▶ *pressure groups*
▶ *dispute resolution*
▶ *online legal advice*

Legal education and training

BUBL Law Sites Index: Legal Education
http://link.bubl.ac.uk:80/ISC4305
This page contains a large number of useful links for legal education. When BUBL started in 1990 the name stood for BUlletin Board for Libraries. Today it is usually just known as the BUBL Information Service, or BUBL for short. BUBL LINK refers to a catalogue of online resources covering all academic subject areas and catalogued according to the traditional Dewey Decimal Classification used by libraries. LINK stands for Libraries of Networked Knowledge. The reviewed links are checked each month.

Fig. 41. BUBL is a well established and respected online resource for students. It covers a huge number of topics from accounting to zoology, as well as law.

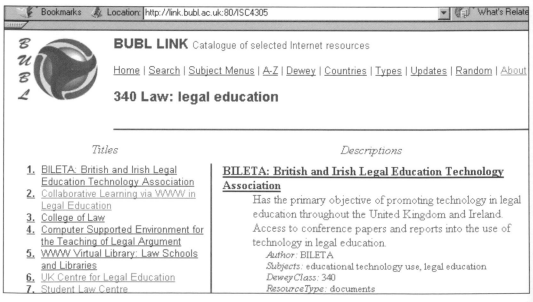

Bookmarks   Location: http://link.bubl.ac.uk:80/ISC4305   What's Relate

BUBL LINK Catalogue of selected Internet resources

Home | Search | Subject Menus | A-Z | Dewey | Countries | Types | Updates | Random | About

340 Law: legal education

Titles	Descriptions
1. BILETA: British and Irish Legal Education Technology Association 2. Collaborative Learning via WWW in Legal Education 3. College of Law 4. Computer Supported Environment for the Teaching of Legal Argument 5. WWW Virtual Library: Law Schools and Libraries 6. UK Centre for Legal Education 7. Student Law Centre	**BILETA: British and Irish Legal Education Technology Association** Has the primary objective of promoting technology in legal education throughout the United Kingdom and Ireland. Access to conference papers and reports into the use of technology in legal education. *Author:* BILETA *Subjects:* educational technology use, legal education *Dewey Class:* 340 *Resource Type:* documents

Chambers & Partners
http://www.chambersandpartners.com/student/
Chambers & Partners are recruitment consultants, who publish a range of legal reference materials. This web page is addressed to the needs of students

College of Law
http://www.lawcol.org.uk
The College of Law 's site welcome students with: 'We're proud to be the leading provider of legal education in England and Wales, and enjoy a growing international reputation. By choosing to study with us, you'll be following in the footsteps of a highly successful elite – more than half of all UK solicitors trained at the College'. The College of Law provides a nationwide coverage, with full-time courses available at four branches in central London, Chester, Guildford and York. Most of the lecturing staff are qualified solicitors or barristers who apply their experience from a range of backgrounds to design and deliver effective and practical training.

Fig. 42. The College of Law web site is an essential resource for would-be solicitors and qualified professionals alike. Check about Lawbytes, its new internet information and graining service.

Department for Education and Employment
http://www.dfee.gov.uk
This is the home page of the Department for Education and Employment (DfEE) site, which publishes a broad range of information about higher education.

Judicial Studies Board
http://www.jsboard.co.uk/
The Judicial Studies Board is the training body of the judiciary in England and Wales. It provides training and instruction for all full-

time and part-time judges in the skills necessary to a judge. An essential element of the philosophy of the JSB is that training is provided by judges for judges. The training requirements of the different jurisdictions are the responsibility of five specialist committees. The JSB also has an advisory role in the training of lay magistrates and of chairmen and members of tribunals.

National Centre for Legal Education
http://www.law.warwick.ac.uk/ncle
This site hosted by the University of Warwick has the web pages of the National Centre for Legal Education.

Student Law Centre
http://www.studentlaw.com
The Student Law Centre has created an excellent site for students covering everything you need to know about how to write the perfect CV and how to handle that crucial interview. There are links to this trainee life, and get a taste of the action as The Student Law Centre goes behind the scenes to see what goes on inside a range of different sized firms. You can do a quick search for a training contract or holiday placement. A very useful site for students.

Trainee Solicitors Group
http://www.tsg.org/
The TSG has around 33,000 members across England and Wales. Membership is free and automatic upon enrollment with the Law Society. It is affiliated to the Law Society from which it receives financial and administrative support. It represents students taking an exempting law degree, a diploma in law, an integrated course studying for the Common Professional Examination, the Legal Practice Course, plus trainee solicitors and solicitors who have been qualified for up to one year.

the trainee
Get all the
latest hot news

Helpline

Check Train Times

The Royal Bank of Scotland
TSG is supported by RBS

UK Institutions Offering Legal Education
http://www.ukcle.ac.uk/tlresources/inst_uk.html
This is an extensive directory of law schools offering undergraduate degrees in the UK. It is maintained by the National Centre for Legal Information at Warwick University.

UK Law Schools
http://www.law.cam.ac.uk/urllists/lawfacul.htm
Produced at the Cambridge University Faculty of Law, this site contains links to over 80 law schools and departments in UK universities and colleges.

University Law Faculties
http://www.smlawpub.co.uk/links/academic.html
This site covers all the UK's law faculties – so you can keep in touch

with your friends. These pages includes handy links to those law faculties who have set up their own web site. Just click to see what courses and facilities are on offer at each. They include:

The University of Aberdeen, University of Abertay Dundee, Anglia Law School, Aston University, Birkbeck College London, the University of Birmingham, Brunel University, University of Buckingham, University of Cambridge, University of Cambridge, Institute of Criminology, Cardiff Law School, University of Central England, University of Central Lancashire, Coventry University, De Montfort University, University of Derby, University of Dundee, University of Durham, University of East Anglia, University of East London, University of Edinburgh, University of Essex, University of Exeter, University of Glamorgan, University of Glasgow, Glasgow Caledonian University, University of Hertfordshire, Huddersfield University, University of Hull, Keele University, University of Kent at Canterbury, King's College, University of Leeds, Leeds Metropolitan University, Leicester University, University of Liverpool, Liverpool John Moores University, London School of Economics, University of Luton, Manchester University, Manchester Metropolitan University, Napier University, Newcastle Law School, University of Nottingham, Nottingham Law School, Nottingham Trent University, University of Oxford, Oxford Brookes University, Plymouth Business School, Queen Mary and Westfield College, University of London, Queen's University of Belfast, University of Reading, Robert Gordon University, School of Oriental and African Studies, London, University of Sheffield, Sheffield Hallam University, South Bank University Business School, University of Southampton, including the Institute of Maritime Law, Southampton Institute, University of Strathclyde, University of Surrey, University of Sussex, University of Teesside, University of Ulster, University College, London, University of Wales Aberystwyth, University of Wales Cardiff, University of Wales Swansea, University of Warwick, University of the West of England, University of Westminster, and the University of Wolverhampton.

Careers

The time soon comes when law students, like all other students, have to contemplate their future, especially their employment and career prospects. Below are some web sites to get you started.

Doctor Job
http://doctorjob.com/thislife/main2.asp
'Graduate careers with attitude.' Find out how a recent graduate finds

a balance between her social life and her job as a trainee lawyer. Follow the link to Career Sectors, then Law. Doctor Job is an online service of GTI which publishes a range of careers handbooks and directories.

Law Careers Net
http://www.lawcareers.net
This is the web site of Law Careers Net. There are links to solicitors' career paths, barristers' career paths, courses, what to learn and where to study, and alternative careers. There are also news and features, information about training contracts and vacation work opportunities, plus real life case studies.

| Bookmarks | Location: | http://www.lawcareers.net/profiles/index.cfm | ▼ | What |

Law Careers.Net

| Brochure Library | Pupillage Mini-Pupillage | Training Contracts Vacation Work | News & Features | Real Life Case Studies |

Real Life Case Studies

This area offers you a slice of what life is really like...

London	Regions	Other	At the Bar
International	South	National Firm	Major London Set
Major City	South West	Tax	Major Provincial Set
Medium City	East Anglia	Consultancy	
Legal Aid	Midlands		
	North		
	Yorkshire &		
	Humberside		

Fig. 43. Law Careers Net is a useful service, maintained by the graduate careers service, Prospects (CSU). There is a newsletter, and a helpful site index.

Law Careers Advice Network
http://www.lcan.csu.ac.uk
LCAN is a partnership of all those involved in providing careers advice to law students and individuals considering a career in law. The network aims to provide all those in careers advice with access to current, accurate and realistic careers information, with the Law Society, the General Council of the Bar and the Institute of Legal Executives acting as a central information point. This site is mainly directed at undergraduates and graduates, but will also be of interest to school students.

Prospects Legal
http://www.prospects.csu.ac.uk
This includes one of the best searchable directories of firms recruiting for vacation work, training contracts and pupillage. From the main

page, follow the Search menu to law opportunities. You can find out about law fairs, courses and postgraduate opportunities, and lots more. Prospects is part of CSU, the Careers Services Unit, which aims to be a UK leader in the development, dissemination and promotion of careers guidance information and recruitment services for Higher Education.

Law libraries

British & Irish Association of Law Librarians
http://www.biall.org.uk/
BIALL was formed in 1969. It is an independent and self-supporting body created to represent the interests of legal information professionals, documentalists and other suppliers of legal literature and reference materials in the United Kingdom and Republic of Ireland.

UK Law Schools and Law Libraries
http://www.law.warwick.ac.uk/cti/lawschools.html
The law schools are listed alphabetically. The links take you directly to the school of law where possible, or to the relevant faculty or department that teaches law, or to the institution's main home page if nothing more specific is available. The links encompass England, Scotland, Wales and Northern Ireland. You can also follow a link to a list of institutions structured according to the type of law courses they offer. The site is maintained by the School of Law at Warwick University.

Fig. 44. UK Law Schools & UK Libraries. This offers a very quick and easy way to check out your possible study options.

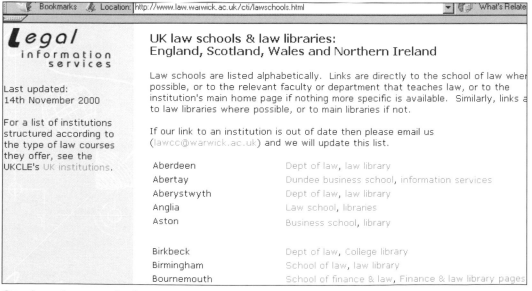

Student law societies

There now follows a selection of UK and other law societies for students.

Law links for students

Bracton Law Society – University of Exeter
http://www.ex.ac.uk/law/
From the Exeter University home page follow the link to the Bracton Law Society.

Cambridge University Law Society
http://www.law.cam.ac.uk/lawsoc/index.htm
They say: 'We arrange barristers' and solicitors' evenings to give students a chance to meet members of the legal profession, prison visits and organise mooting competitions. On the social side we hold the annual Norton Rose Law Ball, cocktails evenings, an annual dinner and, of course, a post-exam garden party, along with various sports matches against teams from City law firms. All our members are kept up to date with a term-card and our official magazine, Per Incuriam'.

Cambridge University Society for Women Lawyers
http://www.cam.ac.uk/societies/cuswl/index.htm
The Society aims to provide a forum for all – law students and non-law students – who want the chance to make their voices heard in the changing legal profession. They say: 'We are a fairly new society – established in 1977 – and hope as a result to be friendly, approachable, and above all useful to anyone looking for guidance in the sometimes intimidating world of law!' They organise workshops to help members perfect the necessary skills, provide opportunities to meet representatives from the bar and major city firms, and to enjoy social occasions.

European Law Students Association
http://www.lns.nl/elsa/
They say: 'Each year since 1981, ELSA has been dedicated to provide opportunities for law students and young lawyers and to assist them to be internationally minded and professionally skilled. Our focus is on encouraging individuals to act for the good of society in order to realise our vision: a just world in which there is respect for human dignity and cultural diversity.' The site is backed by some of the top names in the legal profession, and benefits from a site index.

Glasgow University Law Society
http://www.law.gla.ac.uk/guls/
This is one of the biggest societies in the university, with over 300 members.

International Law Students Association
http://www.ilsa.org/
US-based ILSA has a total membership of over 10,000 throughout the world. Its extensive partnerships with other law student associations reach another 20,000 law students. ILSA membership is made up of chapter memberships and associate memberships. ILSA Chap-

ters mostly consist of International Law Societies at colleges and universities throughout the world. Associate Members are individuals from the community at large interested in international law, mainly pre- and post-law students.

Keele Law Society
http://www.keele.ac.uk/socs/ks19/lawhp.htm
The site offers a range of both academic and careers links.

Law Students Council, University of Edinburgh
http://www.law.ed.ac.uk/lsc/index.htm
There is a link to the University of Edinburgh's School of Law Links Index.

Law Society, School of Oriental and African Studies Department of Law
http://www.soas.ac.uk/Law/soc/home.html

University of Liverpool Bar Society
http://www.liv.ac.uk/~scooper/barsoc.html
The University of Liverpool Bar Society is a student association which aims to aid any students who have decided on a career at the Bar of England and Wales, or who are undecided as to their career and wish to learn more about the profession in order to make a decision either way.

University of Strathclyde Student Law Society
http://law-www-server.law.strath.ac.uk/student/student.html

Pressure groups

Amnesty International
http://www.oneworld.org/amnesty
This is the home page of Amnesty International, the high-profile human rights campaigning organisation. It was launched in 1961 by a British lawyer called Peter Benenson, after he had read about two Portuguese students who had been sentenced to seven years' imprisonment for raising their glasses in a toast to freedom. This is a substantial web site with numerous links, news features and reports.

Institute for Citizenship Studies
http://www.citizen.org.uk
This is an educational project to promote awareness of British and European cjtizenship issues.

Liberty
http://www.liberty.org.uk
Liberty, formerly known as the National Council for Civil Liberties, is

Law links for students ....

news | action | about ai | join us | support ai | education | library | site help

⚖ amnesty international uk

...text-only version

> amnesty news

torture campaign launched

Amnesty International is launching its third major campaign against torture. The first two campaigns – in 1973 and 1984 – brought the extent of torture to the world's attention and are credited with being instrumental in winning final agreement to the UN Convention against Torture. Our latest campaign focuses on the need to bring torturers to justice and and to end the international trade in torture equipment in order to stamp out torture.

| **amnesty works** we've been part of thousands of positive changes since 1961 | **get involved** it doesn't have to take much time or money | **join us online** and make a difference to this world |

> amnesty campaigns

Stamp out torture

Fig. 45. The online home of Amnesty International. Check out the education and library links on the home page.

the leading UK organisation for the defence of civil rights. A notice on the web site in summer 2000 read as follows: 'On and around the weekend of 12-13th August this computer server was subjected to hacker activity aimed at destroying the Campaign's web site. Unfortunately the attempt was successful; the site was deleted, along with about 600 other sites which shared the same file system. The (American) Internet Service Provider has notified the FBI, who have taken the hardware as evidence and are attempting to track down the perpetrators. This site is now running on new equipment with substantially improved security. The information files will hopefully be restored from backup by the ISP shortly.'

Taking Liberties
http://www.tim1.demon.co.uk
Taking Liberties is a UK civil liberties site. It provides some useful news, articles, legal infomation, and reports on demos, campaigns, miscarriages of justice and more.

United Nations Association
http://www.oneworld.org/UNA_UK
The United Nations Association site is worth exploring for news and comment on the work of the UN and its agencies. You will find comment on UK government attitudes and policies on international affairs, overseas aid and more.

Dispute resolution

Since the introduction of the Woolf Reforms, there have been more intense talks about the usage of 'alternative dispute resolution', the so-called methods of ADR: conciliation, mediation and arbitration.

For example, mediation is currently operated under the Family Law Act 1996 in terms of divorce proceedings. Similarly with arbitration, which already exists in employment law matters: pre-employment tribunal hearings are to be extended under the 1998 Employment (Disputes Resolution) Act. Given this growing interest in ADR, listed below is a useful site on ADR for students to explore:

Advisory, Conciliation and Arbitration Service
http://www.acas.org.uk
ACAS maintains an excellent site covering the latest information on ADR, current statistical data, membership of its Council and other information on settling disputes.

Online legal advice

Lastly, online legal services are growing. Below are two sites promising answers to legal queries in a matter of hours or days.

Legal Opinion
http://www.legalopinion.com
This US site provides the user with an online, written opinion from a licensed attorney. It proclaims: 'Whatever your legal question, we can provide you with access to a directory of over 2,300 Attorneys who can help.' With a 'two days response' promise, this service seeks to revolutionise legal advice on the web.

Lawrite
http://www.lawrite.co.uk
Lawrite is a UK example of the fast growing online services. It provides the latest employment law news, facts sheets on many aspects of employment law, CDs on employment law (e.g. contracts, staff

Fig. 46. The Advisory, Conciliation and Arbitration Service (ACAS). It was first established as an independent industrial relations organisation in 1974.

Fig. 47. Legal and financial questions? Contract reviews? Drawing up a will? These and similar services are offered through the web site of Legal Opinion.

handbooks, disciplinary and grievance procedures and discrimination) and other law guides.

▶ *The future* – Will the day come that all legal services are available online?

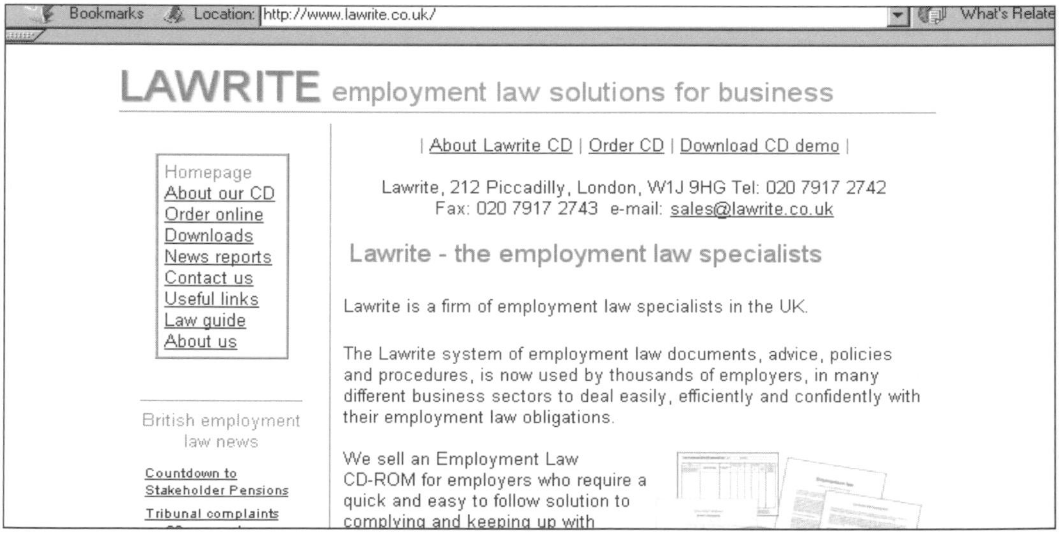

Fig. 48. Lawrite is an established specialist consultancy dealing with employment law in the UK. A CD ROM is available via the web site.

7 A law directory

In this final chapter we explore some web sites for:

▶ *law firms: solicitors*
▶ *law firms: barristers' chambers*
▶ *law networks*
▶ *other learning spaces*

Law firms: solicitors

It would be impossible to list all UK law firms with web sites, so apologies if a particular firm has been missed out. Here is a selection of some of the better known ones:

Addleshaw Booth & Co
http://www.addleshaw.booth.co.uk
Addleshaw Booth & Co acts for 36 of the FTSE 250 companies and 42 of The Times top 200 quoted companies. Its clients include 3i plc, Airtours, British Aerospace, British Vita, BT, the Ministry of Defence, Railtrack, Trinity International Holdings and AAH. It has around 100 partners, a further 180 lawyers and more than 200 other fee-earners.

Fig. 49. The web site of top UK solicitors Allen & Overy includes details of its various practice areas.

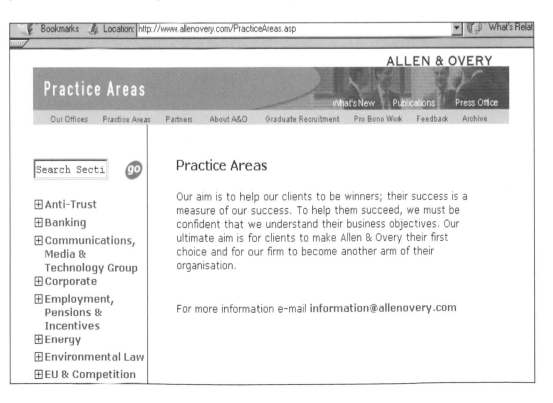

A law directory

Allen & Overy
http://www.allenovery.com
http://www.newchange.com
Founded in 1930, Allen & Overy is a premier London-based international law firm with 268 partners and over 3,000 staff working in 23 major centres worldwide.

Ashurst Morris Crisp
http://www.ashursts.co.uk
Ashursts has been providing legal services for more than 175 years. It recently ranked third in a survey of UK law firms with the highest number of clients listed on the London Stock Exchange. The site contains details of its practice areas, recruitment and publications.

Baker and McKenzie,
http://www.bakernet.com/
Founded in 1949 Baker and McKenzie is a City of London law firm of over 170 lawyers offering a broad range of services. The firm offers access to its library services and various commercial and legal databases, and internal and external communication through its proprietary BakerNet email and other networks.

Barlow Lyde & Gilbert
http://www.blg.co.uk
With over 70 partners, the firm advises corporate organisations, government bodies, financial and other institutions in all spheres of business activity, from its offices in the City of London Hong Kong, and at Lloyd's. It is well known for its work in litigation and other forms of dispute resolution. The firm offers around 15 training contracts each year.

Beachcroft Wansbroughs
http://www.vaudreys.com/
With an annual income of more than £65m, the firm's services are based upon specific client market sectors, mainly in the commercial, health and insurance arenas.

Berrymans Lace Mawer
http://www.blm-law.com
The firm has what may be the largest insurance litigation practice in the UK. Over 80 per cent of its work involves advising the insurance market and the firm has one of the UK's largest personal injury practices. It has branches in Birmingham, Leeds, Liverpool, London, Manchester, Southampton and Dubai, and a staff of more than 700 worldwide.

S J Berwin & Co
http://www.sjberwin.com/

Founded in 1982, S J Berwin & Co acts for clients from major multi-national business corporations and financial institutions to high-net-worth individuals. The firm has a number of leading entrepreneurial business clients. It maintains offices in London, Brussels and Frankfurt, and has earnings of around £55m a year.

Berwin Leighton
http://www.berwinleighton.com/
http://www.t@xandlegal.com
Berwin Leighton is a London-based law firm with a recognised expertise in property, finance and corporate law.

Cameron McKenna
http://www.cmh.co.uk/
http://www.cmck.com
Cameron McKenna has joined forces with five other top European law firms to create CMS, a transnational legal services organisation. The group has 31 offices in 19 jurisdictions in Europe, the CIS, Asia-Pacific and North America and is committed to providing clients with integrated, seamless services. See also its legal updating service at:

http://www.cmck.com

Clifford Chance
http://www.CliffordChance.com/
http://www.nextlaw.com
Over the years, Clifford Chance has grown into an international, multi-jurisdictional law firm handling all aspects of business and finance,

Fig. 50. Clifford Chance is using internet technology to develop a range of new online services.

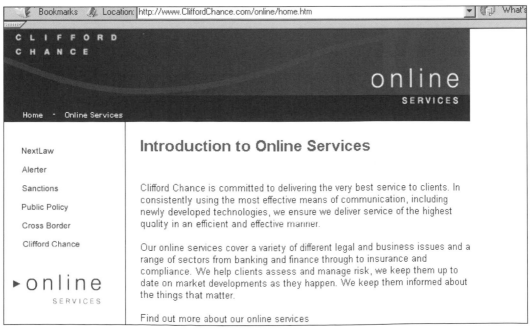

and today grossing some £400m a year in fees. In January 2000 it merged with Rogers & Wells LLP and Pünder, Volhard, Weber & Axster to create Clifford Chance LLP, an integrated global law firm designed to meet the needs of businesses operating in the international market. It is one of the largest law firms in the world with over 3,000 legal advisers

Clyde & Co
http://www.clydeco.com
The site includes legal opinions on current world events. Company background and a directory of more than 100 partners, consultants and senior associates can be found here. There are interactive elements, a regular magazine section and some online archives. Students considering a legal career can check out background information and contact details in its careers section. There is also a useful set of links to online legal, financial, and information resources.

Davies Arnold Cooper
http://www.dac.co.uk
Established in 1927, the firm is active in the insurance, financial services, construction, commercial property, pharmaceutical, healthcare and retail industries. It has 50 partners and over 430 staff, with offices in London, Manchester, Newcastle, and Madrid. Its web site is offered as an information resource, with sections highlighting key developments updated regularly. A keyword search helps you find what you want quickly and easily.

Denton Hall
http://www.dentonhall.com
http://www.dentonwildsapte.com
Denton Hall (Denton Wilde Sapte) is a prominent general service business law firm with offices around the world. It offers a comprehensive range of commercial legal advice and is strong in banking and finance, energy and infrastructure, media and technology, property, retail and aviation. The firm is a founder member of Denton International which, with Denton Wilde Sapte, has 33 offices in 21 jurisdictions around the world.

Dibb Lupton Alsop
http://www.dla-law.co.uk
Dibb Lupton Alsop is one of the UK's top ten law firms. The site features recent news and a news archive, free publications, recruitment, training, ecommerce and other services. All the firm's locations are equipped with video-conferencing facilities, ensuring that clients and partners can speak quickly when necessary.

Edge Ellison
http://www.edge.co.uk/

The Edge Ellison partnership has corporate, commercial property, and construction and engineering departments, and deals also with litigation, pensions and finance law. The firm employs over 600 people and has an annual fee income of around £35m.

Eversheds
http://www.eversheds.com
A European law firm, Eversheds has 1,500 legal and business advisers based in 19 locations. Its specialist services encompass business risk services, computer/IT, corporate tax, environment, health and safety, EU and competition law, franchising, insolvency, intellectual property, international public law, licensing, PFI, planning, pensions, private capital and tax matters, and venture capital.

Field Fisher Waterhouse
http://www.ffwlaw.com.
This London firm's client base includes commercial and industrial companies, banks and other financial institutions, governments, trade associations, regulatory bodies and professional partnerships. It also acts for a substantial number of overseas clients and has good links with China, France, Germany, Italy, Japan, Korea, Scandinavia and the US.

D J Freeman
http://www.cygnet.co.uk/DJFreeman/
This London-based firm specialises in internet and media law. This page offers some useful guidance notes about the legal implications of the internet viewed from a UK perspective.

Fig. 51. The web site of Freshfields Bruckhaus Deringer.

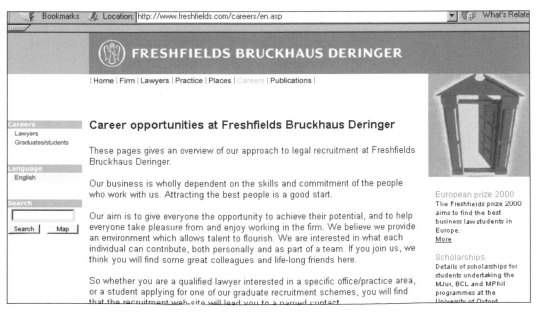

95

A law directory ....

Freshfields Bruckhaus Deringer
http://www.freshfields.com
Freshfields is an old-established international law firm with a network of 30 offices across Europe, Asia and the US, providing a comprehensive worldwide service to national and multinational corporations, financial institutions and governments. A market leader in international transactions, the firm also has a top domestic practice in many countries.

Gouldens
http://www.gouldens.com
With earnings of around £28m, Gouldens is a leading corporate firm based in the City of London. Its specialist groups cover areas such as corporate tax, international and personal tax planning, environment, IP, IT, employment, employee benefits and pensions, regulatory matters, fraud and white collar crime. Languages spoken include Dutch, French, German, Greek, Hebrew, Italian, Japanese, Romanian, Russian, Spanish, Welsh and Czech.

Hammond Suddards
http://www.hammondsuddards.com
http://www.hammondsuddardsedge.com
Hammond Suddards acts for public and large private companies, banks, building societies, insurance companies and a wide range of financial and other institutions.

Fig. 52. Herbert Smith & Co has emerged as one of the top City of London based law firms in recent years.

Herbert Smith
http://www.herbertsmith.com
Founded in 1882, Herbert Smith has developed into a premier inter-

national law firm operating from the City of London, Brussels, Paris, Bangkok, Hong Kong and Singapore. It employs over 725 lawyers and another 700 support staff. It grosses over £140m in fees each year. Its areas of specialism include: administrative and public law, banking, civil fraud, construction, defamation, employment, energy, environment, information technology, insurance and reinsurance, intellectual property, public and private international law, professional indemnity, regulatory and compliance cases, and sport.

Holman Fenwick & Willan
email@hfw.co.uk
Founded in 1883, HF&W is an international law firm and specialist in maritime transportation, insurance, reinsurance and trade. The firm is a leader in the field of commercial litigation and arbitration and also offers comprehensive commercial and financial advice. It has a network of offices covering London, Paris, Rouen, Nantes, Piraeus, Hong Kong, Shanghai and Singapore.

Ince
http://www.ince.co.uk
Ince specialises in maritime and insurance law, and has been involved in some major cases of maritime disasters and environmental pollution. It operates a 24-hour emergency response service 365 days a year in respect of maritime, aviation and energy related casualties. It handles cases covering all aspects of international trade, from its offices in the City of London, Hong Kong, Singapore, and Piraeus.

Irwin Mitchell
http://www.irwinmitchell.co.uk
Established over 80 years ago, Sheffield-based Irwin Mitchell specialises in general commercial and litigation work, housing association and public sector work, personal injury, medical negligence and product liability work, and work for private clients. It has 74 partners and over 1,000 staff.

K-legal
http://www.klegal.com
A newly formed law firm, combining lawyers, accountants and management consultants.

Lawrence Graham
http://www.lawgram.com/
The 400-strong firm is based in London and its business is organised into four main practice areas: commercial property, corporate/commercial, litigation, and tax and financial management. The commercial property department is the largest in the firm. The firm also has an office in the Ukraine where it has had clients since the 1920s.

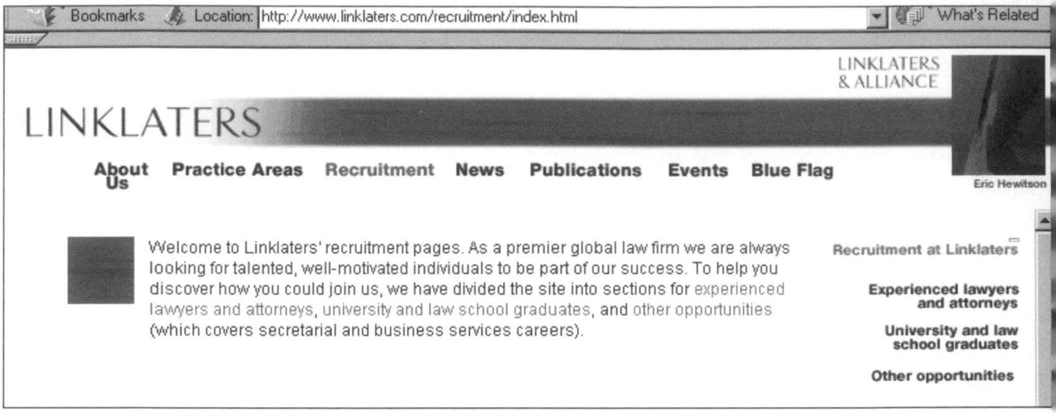

A law directory ....

Fig. 53. The recruitment
section of Linklaters'
web site.

Linklaters & Alliance
http://www.linklaters.com/
http://www.blueflag.com
Established more than 150 years ago, Linklaters is generally regarded as one of the world's premier global law firms, operating from the UK and major financial centres around the world. The firm offers a full range of legal services in corporate work, international finance, commercial property, litigation, IP, technology, communications and tax. It is a member of Linklaters & Alliance which comprises five of Europe's leading law firms.

Lovells
http://www.lovellwhitedurrant.com/
http://www.lovells.com
Lovell White Durrant is a European-based international law firm operating worldwide from offices in London, Chicago, New York, Paris, Brussels, Prague, Ho Chi Minh City, Hong Kong, Beijing and Tokyo.

Macfarlanes
http://www.macfarlanes.com/
The partnership works with clients in industrial and commercial sectors. Its main areas of practice are company commercial and banking, property, litigation, and tax and financial planning. It has 54 partners and a staff of around 420. It publishes a range of practice notes, newsletters, and guidance notes for clients.

Masons
http://www.masons.com/
http://www.out-law.com
Established over 50 years ago, Masons' London operation is supported by a regional network of offices in Leeds, Manchester, Bristol and Glasgow. International matters are handled by Masons' offices in Brussels, Dublin, Hong Kong, Guangzhou (China) and Singapore.

The firm is noted for its services to the computer, infrastructure, and engineering and construction industries.

Merriman White
http://www.merrimanwhite.co.uk/
This London firm specialises in medical, injury, patents, consumer, company and commercial law. They say: 'We have been established since 1740 and based in King's Bench Walk from that time.' Its web site offers a 'free assessment of your personal injury claim'.

Morgan Cole
http://www.morgan-cole.com/
Morgan Cole is located along the M4 corridor. It has a fee income in excess of £30m, and seven offices in London, the Thames Valley and South Wales providing a service to commercial clients across the UK.

Nabarro Nathanson
http://www.nabarro.com/
This leading firm has more than 100 partners and approximately 350 other lawyers working in offices in London, Reading and Sheffield, as well as Brussels where it has a specialist EU and competition law unit. The site includes illustrated partner profiles.

Norton Rose
http://www.nortonrose.com
Norton Rose is a major international law firm with its principal office in the City of London and a worldwide network of offices from Athens to Bangkok. It acts for banks and other financial institutions, international businesses, major public and private companies, government departments and sovereign states. The company is particularly active in corporate finance, debt, asset and project finance, banking and capital markets, and company and commercial law. The web site includes a section of career opportunities, and a legal resources room.

Trainee Solicitors

Legal

Non-legal

Contact us

Press Release search

Site search

Olswang
http://www.olswang.co.uk/
http://www.olswang.com
Olswang provides corporate, commercial, property and litigation advice to the media, communications, entertainment and technology sectors in the UK and overseas. Formed in 1981, it now has 47 partners, 189 lawyers, and 222 support staff. It operates a 'dress down Friday' policy.

Pannone & Partners
http://ww.pannonecom
A Manchester-based law firm.

A law directory ....

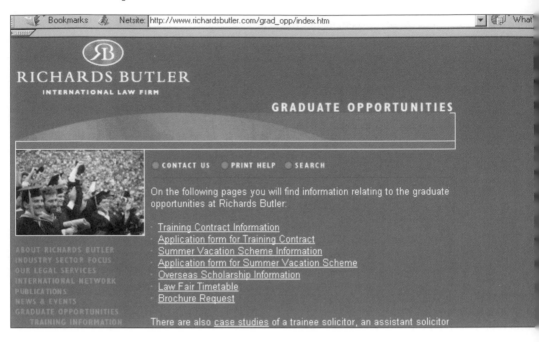

Netsite: http://www.richardsbutler.com/grad_opp/index.htm

RICHARDS BUTLER
INTERNATIONAL LAW FIRM

GRADUATE OPPORTUNITIES

● CONTACT US   ● PRINT HELP   ● SEARCH

On the following pages you will find information relating to the graduate
opportunities at Richards Butler:

- Training Contract Information
- Application form for Training Contract
- Summer Vacation Scheme Information
- Application form for Summer Vacation Scheme
- Overseas Scholarship Information
- Law Fair Timetable
- Brochure Request

ABOUT RICHARDS BUTLER
INDUSTRY SECTOR FOCUS
OUR LEGAL SERVICES
INTERNATIONAL NETWORK
PUBLICATIONS
NEWS & EVENTS
GRADUATE OPPORTUNITIES
   TRAINING INFORMATION

There are also case studies of a trainee solicitor, an assistant solicitor

Fig. 54. Graduate
opportunities at
Richards Butler.

Pinsent Curtis
http://www.pinsents.com/
The firm combines a strong City of London operation with major
offices in the principal business centres of the UK. It has around 130
partners and 800 staff operating from offices in London, Birmingham,
Leeds and Brussels. The web site includes links to meet the partners,
and recruitment.

Richards Butler
http://www.richardsbutler.com/
With over 1,000 staff worldwide, the London-based firm acts mainly
for larger international clients concerned with banking and financial
services; commodity trading; insurance; media, entertainment and
leisure; information technology and telecommunications; shipping;
and property. More than half its work has an international dimension.

Rowe and Maw
http://www.roweandmaw.co.uk/
Founded over 100 years ago, Rowe & Maw is one of the UK's leading
commercial law firms, based in the City of London. It also advise
clients internationally, either through its EU and competition law
office in Brussels or through a well established network of contacts,

Shoosmiths
http://www.shoosmiths.co.uk
The practice of this regional firm comprises six main sectors: business
services, property services, financial institutions, banking, personal

injury, and private client. Its gross fee income is around £36m, and it has a staff of around 1,000 people.

Simmons and Simmons
http://www.elexica.com
http://www.simmons-simmons.com/elexica.htm
Simmons and Simmons, the international law firm, offers free internet access for students and lawyers. This site aspires to build an online legal community for its clients. It offers not only newsletters, online checklists and links, but also discussion forums. It has offices in Europe, Asia, and the United States.

Slaughter & May
http://www.slaughterandmay.com
Slaughter and May is a leading and old-established English law firm with a very large international corporate, commercial and financial practice. It has a worldwide staff of over 1,200 including some 600 lawyers. There is a section on careers which includes a brief preview of the firm and its practice, details of career opportunities, and vacation schemes, and how to make an application to join the firm. You can also apply online for a graduate opportunities brochure.

Stephenson Harwood
http://www.StephensonHarwood.com
The firm specialises in corporate finance, banking, property, and a high-profile litigation and arbitration practice. It is one of the few leading City of London law firms that still undertakes private client, family and matrimonial work.

Taylor Joynson Garrett
http://www.tjg.co.uk
Taylor Joynson Garrett is a prominent City of London law firm. It produces regular updates on various legal issues which can be accessed via this web site. It is ranked among the top thirty law firms in London, having over 450 staff, 240 lawyers and 82 partners.

Theodore Goddard
http://www.theogoddard.com
Founded in 1902, Theodore Goddard is today a premier City of London-based firm with many famous clients. It advises on all aspects of business-related law, in particular banking, finance, music, broadcasting, theatre, film and television, property, publishing, and employment. They say that their modern approach is backed by a solid investment in information technology, highly effective communications systems and training at all levels.

A law directory

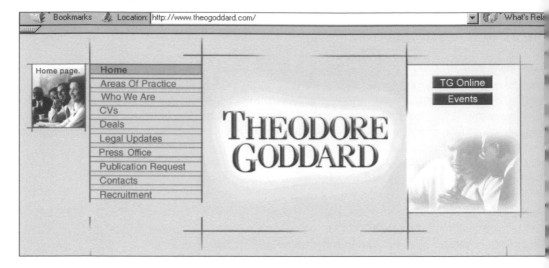

Fig. 55. Theodore Goddard. You can apply for a training contract in writing or by email, and check out the online CVs of its own partners.

Thompsons
http://www.thompsons.law.co.uk
Since 1921, Thompsons has grown into one of the largest personal injury practices in the UK. It has a national network of 14 offices. The firm only acts for claimants' personal injury work and for employees in employment and criminal matters. It regularly secures more than £100,000 in compensation amounts for clients. The firm also undertakes conditional fee work.

Titmuss Sainer Dechert
http://www.titmuss-sainer-dechert.com
The firm serves commercial, industrial, property, financial, and individual clients in a range of specialties, including retail, litigation, and financial services.

Travers Smith Braithwaite
http://www.traverssmith.co.uk
With over 160 lawyers, London-based Travers Smith Braithwaite is one of the UK's leading corporate, financial and commercial law firms. The impressively fast-loading site includes details of professional and graduate recruitment. You can click on links to read three case studies involving trainee solicitors at the firm.

Watson, Farley & Williams
http://www.wfw.com/
Founded in 1982, this is an international commercial law firm specialising in shipping and aircraft finance, litigation, and general corporate law. Based in the City of London, it has offices worldwide. Its staff can advise on English, French, Russian, New York and US federal laws.

Wragge & Co
http://www.wragge.co.uk/
Birmingham-based Wragge & Co provides a comprehensive service for major companies, public authorities and financial institutions, in the UK and overseas, including over 165 listed companies. About a fifth of its work is international. Its fee income amounts to some £50m and its major clients include BA, PowerGen, Severn Trent, Cadbury Schweppes, and AT&T.

Barristers chambers

This is a cross-section of barristers' chambers which have developed an online presence. The chambers are based both inside and outside London, and cover a variety of legal disciplines.

1 Mitre Court Buildings
http://www.1mitrecourt.com/
This is a specialist set of chambers in which all members practise exclusively in the field of family law. They offer a range of services covering financial relief, care proceedings, adoption, child abduction and more. There are currently seven QCs and 23 junior barristers. Among former members of chambers are Lord Simon of Glaisdale and Lady Justice Butler-Sloss. They say: 'Most members of Cham bers have their own personal computers and can provide documents on disk or by email. All members of Chambers belong to the Family Law Bar Association.'

One King's Bench Walk
http://www.1kbw.co.uk
They say: 'We are an established set of chambers with members at all levels of seniority who between them undertake a broad range of work. Many of them contribute to specialist publications: members currently include two editors of Jackson and Davies Matrimonial Finance and Taxation, and an author of Hershman and McFarlane's Children Law and Practice and two editors of Archbold's Criminal Pleading, Evidence and Practice. We have strong specialist groups in family law, criminal law and general common law as well as individual expertise in many other areas of work.'

No 6 Barristers Chambers
http://www.no6.co.uk
These are Leeds-based chambers specialising in family, chancery and commercial, criminal, personal injury, and professional negligence law. The site includes detailed barristers' profiles, linked to their various areas of specialism.

12 New Square Barristers' Chambers
http://www.12newsquare.co.uk/
The chambers' members specialise in chancery and commercial law.

They say: 'This new set is now one of the largest in Lincoln's Inn, offering the services of 9 silks and 35 junior counsel, with skills covering the full range of chancery and commercial practice at every level of seniority.' The site includes links to barristers, administration, practice, cases, pupillage, maps and travel, legal news, a day calculator, and search facility.

24 Old Buildings
http://www.24oldBuildings.law.co.uk/
This set of Chancery Chambers was formed over 25 years ago. They say: 'Since then, Chambers has developed to reflect the changes that have taken place in the Chancery field and it now offers the specialist expertise required for a wide range of commercial and equity disputes and problems. Members of Chambers have been involved in some of the most widely reported cases of the last ten years, involving such well-known names as BCCI, Maxwell and Barings.'

Durham Barristers Chambers
http://www.durhambarristers.com/
They say: 'Established in 1996 by local practitioners, chambers has grown and developed distinct specialisations. Common law matters, crime, civil and commercial law are important areas of work. Planning, environmental and local government law have been specialisations from the outset.' The site includes barristers' profiles.

Fig. 56. Details of pupillage can be found at the web site of New Square Chambers.

Essex Court Chambers
http://www.essexcourt-chambers.law.co.uk/
Its specialist areas include: administrative law and judicial review, agriculture and farming, arbitration, aviation banking, Chinese law, company law and insolvency, conflict of laws, construction and, en-

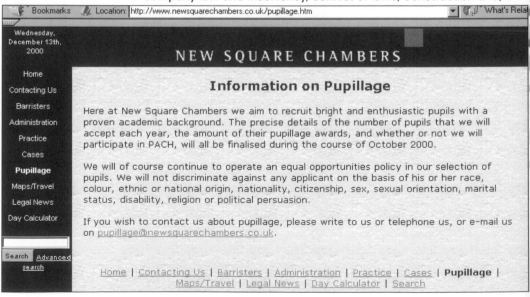

Bookmarks   Location: http://www.newsquarechambers.co.uk/pupillage.htm   What's Relal

Wednesday,
December 13th,
2000

NEW SQUARE CHAMBERS

Home
Contacting Us
Barristers
Administration
Practice
Cases
Pupillage
Maps/Travel
Legal News
Day Calculator

Search Advanced
search

Information on Pupillage

Here at New Square Chambers we aim to recruit bright and enthusiastic pupils with a proven academic background. The precise details of the number of pupils that we will accept each year, the amount of their pupillage awards, and whether or not we will participate in PACH, will all be finalised during the course of October 2000.

We will of course continue to operate an equal opportunities policy in our selection of pupils. We will not discriminate against any applicant on the basis of his or her race, colour, ethnic or national origin, nationality, citizenship, sex, sexual orientation, marital status, disability, religion or political persuasion.

If you wish to contact us about pupillage, please write to us or telephone us, or e-mail us on pupillage@newsquarechambers.co.uk.

Home | Contacting Us | Barristers | Administration | Practice | Cases | **Pupillage** |
Maps/Travel | Legal News | Day Calculator | Search

gineering, commodity transactions, computer law, employment law, energy and utilities law, entertainment and sports law, environmental law, European law, financial services, human rights, injunctions and arrests, insurance and reinsurance, international trade and transport, professional negligence, public international law, public law, sale of goods and product liability, shipping, VAT and excise. The original founding members were Michael Kerr (later Lord Justice Kerr), Robert MacCrindle, Michael Mustill (later Lord Mustill), Anthony Evans (later Lord Justice Evans), and Anthony Diamond (later Judge Diamond), all of whom at some time headed Chambers.

Guildford Chambers
http://www.guildfordbarristers.com/
They say: 'Guildford Chambers was established in 1976 as a small annexe of a London set, in the belief that solicitors in the area would welcome the service available from local chambers. That expectation was amply justified and since 1981 Guildford Chambers has been completely independent. In recent years it has expanded rapidly and there are now eighteen barristers, including one Queen's Counsel.'

Old Square Chambers
http://www.oldsquarechambers.co.uk/index.html
Its barristers specialise in employment law, environmental law, personal injury and clinical negligence, and product liability law. Detailed members' profiles are included, along with a useful page of legal hyperlinks, and information about pupillage.

Trinity Chambers
http://www.trinitychambers.co.uk/
These are barristers' chambers in Newcastle upon Tyne, with principle areas of practice in chancery, commercial, common law, crime, employment, family, and licensing. They say: 'Chambers is the first set north of London, and only the fourth in England and Wales, to gain the British Standard Institutions' accreditation of BarMark, which was ratified by the General Council of the Bar on 10th April 2000.'

Law networks

ALeRT UK
http://www.alertuk.com
ALeRT UK (UK) is a group of law firms dedicated exchanging information.

LawGroup
http://www.lawgroup.co.uk/
The LawGroup UK is a national network of independent solicitors' firms. It was launched in 1988 to provide a response to the challenge facing independent firms, and since then has continued to grow.

A law directory

Today it comprises over 60 practices throughout the UK with a combined fee income of over £150 million. All have a diverse client range and specific areas of expertise. Member firms can draw on the experience of more than 600 partners and 2,000 staff in over 100 locations. LawGroup says it selects firms who are committed to continual improvement, focusing on client service and quality. Its solicitors are developing new expertise in the fast growing and niche areas of the law, as well as improving their skills and approach to traditional areas of practice.

LawNet
http://www.lawnet-uk.com
LawNet provides details on law firms in many locations throughout the United Kingdom, the Republic of Ireland and the Channel Islands. Its online services provide information about the practice of law – using a lawyer, and the work undertaken. The addresses of relevant authorities, associations and national institutions can also be found by following links on the site.

International Centre for Commercial Law (ICC Law)
http://www.icclaw.com/l500/uk.htm
Here you can explore the well-known Legal 500 Series: The Legal 500, The European Legal 500, The Asia Pacific Legal 500, and The Legal 500, which provides a detailed guide to UK law firms. The Legal 500 was first published in 1988 and has grown to be the definitive client reference to the UK's commercial law firms. The Times newspaper has described The Legal 500 as 'the bible of the legal business.' The Legal 500 is the most used and most referred to legal directory, with 89 per cent of senior company lawyers using it each year (Gallup). Each year over 20,000 copies are printed and the information is also made available on the internet site (the International Centre for Commercial Law). A team of experienced researchers present reviews of over 80 individual practice areas and assess the strengths of the firms in these fields. The regions are covered in the same way and a section covering the Bar was added in the 1996 edition. The online version of The Legal 500 is available from this web page.

links page
Links to our favourite
websites and firms

Logos
http://www.logos-eeig.com
Logos is a network of independent law firms in Europe. With one law firm in each of twelve countries of the European Union and contacts in the other three, Logos can assist any business or law firm around the world that needs legal support in Europe.

case tracker
Keep up to date on the
progress of your case

National Solicitors Network
http://www.tnsn.com/
National Solicitors Network is a network of independent solicitors' practices with over 500 member offices throughout England and

legal surgery

Wales which is setting new standards in the provision of high quality, reasonably priced, legal services to private, institutional and corporate clients.

Fig. 57. The Legal 500 is an essential resource for career planning and progression. You can check out the Legal 500 at the ICC Law web site.

Lawyers on the Web
http://www.infolaw.co.uk/ifl/lawyers.htm
Lawyers on the Web is a useful and comprehensive guide to law firms, solicitors and law organisations which have launched internet pages.

Other learning spaces

Lastly, many organisations, particularly management consultants, have web sites which provide up-to-date information on all sorts and ranges of topics, and online professional services. For example:

KnowledgeSpace
http://www.knowledgespace.com
Arthur Andersen's KnowledgeSpace is an example of an 'online community' offering professional services.

Reuters
http://www.reuters.com/news
This site is Reuters, the news agency, interface with online quick access to the latest international news and events.

The final word!

Good luck in your legal studies on and off the web....Happy surfing!
Remember, web access could be the key to your success!

Appendix: Law publishers and booksellers

Law publishers

Blackstone Press
http://www.blackstonepress.co.uk/
Catalogue, legal links

Butterworths LEXIS Direct
http://www.butterworths.com
Catalogue, news direct, New Law Journal, legal links, LEXIS-NEXIS
Professional

Cameron May
http://neon.airtime.co.uk/C-May/

Cavendish
http://www.cavendishpublishing.com/

Context
http://www.context.co.uk/navigate/main.asp
Product information, link to JUSTIS.com, daily UK law news

Hart Publishing
http://www.hartpub.co.uk/

HMSO
http://www.hmso.gov.uk
Legislation, copyright information

Incorporated Council of Law Reporting
http://www.lawreports.co.uk
Catalogue, recent case reports, Daily Law Notes service

Jordan Publishing
http://www.familylaw.co.uk/html/jordan_publishing.html
Catalogue, legal links

Kluwer
http://www.kluwerlaw.com
Catalogue, new and forthcoming publications

Lawtel
http://www.lawtel.co.uk
Online legal information database

Appendix: Law publishers and booksellers

Oxford University Press
http://www1.oup.co.uk/academic/Law/

Palladian Law Publishing
http://www.palladianlaw.com/

Sweet & Maxwell
http://www.smlawpub.co.uk
Catalogue, UK and EU daily alerters, legal links, civil procedure rules
online

The Stationery Office Official Documents
http://www.official-documents.co.uk/menu/ukpinf.htm
Publications on the Internet from HMSO, The Stationery Office, UK
Parliament and government departments.

Tolley
http://www.butterworths.co.uk/tolley/cat.htm

Law booksellers

Hammicks Legal Bookshops Online
http://www.hammicks-bookshops.co.uk/
A very good online bookshop for UK law books with an easy search
interface. Normally a better way to find bibliographic information on
law books than searching the publishers' websites above.

Lawyers' Professional Book Services
http://www.lawbooks.freeserve.co.uk
A good source of up to date information on British law books, lists of
new editions, all with easy to see bibliographic details.

Law journals

Electronic law journals - Warwick University
http://elj.warwick.ac.uk/
This handy site includes information on and links to all the main UK
law journals as well as to numerous other resources

European Journal of International Law
http://www.ejil.org/
For volume 1 (1990) onwards.

Law Society's Gazette
http://www.lawgazette.co.uk/
Here you can view the current issue and explore an archive of the
current year.

Appendix: Law publishers and booksellers............................

The Lawyer
http://www.the-lawyer.co.uk/
This is the online version of the legal practitioners' newspaper.

On Line Law Review
http://www.solent.ac.uk/law/ollr.html
This is also from Southampton Institute, a student-edited journal.

Student Law Review
http://www.cavendishpublishing.com/cavmaster.html
This is now available on the Cavendish Publishing site

Glossary of internet terms

access provider – The company that provides you with access to the internet. This may be an independent provider or a large international organisation such as AOL or CompuServe. See also **internet service provider**.

ActiveX – A Microsoft programming language that allows effects such as animations, games and other interactive features to be included a web page.

Adobe Acrobat – A type of software required for reading PDF files (' portable document format'). You may need to have Adobe Acrobat Reader when downloading large text files from the internet, such as lengthy reports or chapters from books. If your computer lacks it, the web page will prompt you, and usually offer you an immediate download of the free version.

address book – A directory in a web browser where you can store people's email addresses. This saves having to type them out each time you want to email someone. You just click on an address whenever you want it.

ADSL – Asymmetric Digital Subscriber Line, a new phone line technology which provides an internet connection speed up to 10 times faster than a typical modem.

affiliate programme – A system that allows you to sell other companies products via your web site.

AltaVista – One of the half dozen most popular internet search engines. Just type in a few key words to find what you want on the internet. See: www.altavista.com

AOL – America On Line, the world's biggest internet service provider, with more than 25 million subscribers, and now merged with Time Warner. Because it has masses of content of its own - quite aside from the wider internet - it is sometimes referred to as an ' online' service provider rather than internet service provider. It has given away vast numbers of free CDs with the popular computer magazines to build its customer base. It also owns Netscape. See: www.aol.com

Apple Macintosh – A type of computer that has its own proprietary operating system, as distinct from the MSDOS and Windows operating systems found on PCs (personal computers). The Apple Mac has long been a favourite of designers and publishers.

applet – An application programmed in Java that is designed to run only on a web browser. Applets cannot read or write data onto your computer, only from the domain in which they are served from. When a web page using an applet is accessed, the browser will download it and run it on your computer. See also **Java**.

application – Any program, such as a word processor or spreadsheet program, designed to carry out a task on your computer.

application service provider – A company that provides computer software via the internet, whereby the application is borrowed, rather than downloaded. You keep your data, they keep the program.

ARPANET – Advanced Research Projects Agency Network, an early form of the internet in the USA in the 1960s.

ASCII – American Standard Code for Information Interchange. It is a simple text file format that can be accessed by most word processors and text editors. It is a universal file type for passing textual information across the internet.

Ask Jeeves – A popular internet search engine. Rather than just typing in a few key words for your search, you can type in a whole question or instruction, such as 'Find me everything about employment law.' It draws on a database of millions of questions and answers, and works best with fairly general questions.

Glossary of internet terms ....

ASP – (1) Active server page, a filename extension for a type of web page. (2) Application service provider (see above).

attachment – A file sent with an email message. The attached file can be anything from a word-processed document to a database, spreadsheet, graphic, or even a sound or video file. For example you could email someone birthday greetings, and attach a sound track or video clip.

Authenticode – Authenticode is a system where ActiveX controls can be authenticated in some way, usually by a certificate.

avatar – A cartoon or image used to represent someone on screen while taking part in internet chat.

backup – A second copy of a file or a set of files. Backing up data is essential if there is any risk of data loss.

bandwidth – The width of the electronic highway that gives you access to the internet. The higher the bandwidth, the wider this highway, and the faster the traffic can flow.

banner ad – This is a band of text and graphics, usually situated at the top of a web page. It acts like a title, telling the user what the content of the page is about. It invites the visitor to click on it to visit that site. Banner advertising has become big business.

baud rate – The data transmission speed in a modem, measured in bps (bits per second).

BBS – Bulletin board service. A method of reading and posting public messages at a particular web site.

binary numbers – The numbering system used by computers. It only uses 1s and 0s to represent numbers. Decimal numbers are based on the number 10. You can count from nought to nine. When you count higher than nine, the nine is replaced with a 10. Binary numbers are based on the number 2: each place can only have the value of 1 or 0.

Blue Ribbon Campaign – A widely supported campaign supporting free speech and opposing moves to censor the internet by all kinds of elected and unelected bodies. See the Electronic Frontier Foundation at: www.eff.org

bookmark – A file of URLs of your favourite internet sites. Bookmarks are very easily created by bookmarking (mouse-clicking) any internet page you like the look of. If you are an avid user, you could soon end up with hundreds of them! In the Internet Explorer browser and AOL they are called Favorites.

Boolean search – A search in which you type in words such as AND and OR to refine your search. Such words are called 'Boolean operators'. The concept is named after George Boole, a nineteenth-century English mathematician.

bot – Short for robot. It is used to refer to a program that will perform a task on the internet, such as carrying out a search.

browser Your browser is your window to the internet, and will normally supplied by your internet service provider when you first sign up. It is the program that you use to access the world wide web, and manage your personal communications and privacy when online. By far the two most popular browsers are Microsoft Internet Explorer and Netscape Communicator. You can easily swap, or use both. Both can be downloaded free from their web sites (a lengthy process) and are found on the CD roms stuck to the computer magazines. It won't make much difference which one you use - they both do much the same thing. Opera (www.opera.com) is an alternative, as is NetCaptor (www.netcaptor.com). America Online (www.aol.com) has its own proprietary browser which is not available separately.

bug – A weakness in a program or a computer system. They are remedied by ' fixes' or ' patches' which can be downloaded.

bulletin board – A type of computer-based news service that provides an email service and a file archive.

Add Bookmark
File Bookmark
Edit Bookmarks...

Books & publishing
Business
Collecting
Directories
Education
Entertainment
Help
Internet

cache – A file storage area on a computer. Your web browser will normally cache (copy to your hard drive) each web page you visit. When you revisit that page on the web, you may in fact be looking at the page originally cached on your computer. To be sure you are viewing the current page, press **reload** or **refresh** on your browser toolbar. You can empty your cache from time to time, and the computer will do so automatically whenever the cache is full. In Internet Explorer, pages are saved in the Windows folder, Temporary Internet Files. In Netscape they are saved in a folder called Cache.

certificate – A computer file that securely identifies a person or organisation on the internet.

CGI – Common gateway interface. This defines how the web server should pass information to the program, such as what it's being asked to do, what objects it should work with, any inputs, and so on. It is the same for all web servers.

channel (chat) – Place where you can chat with other internet chatters. The name of a chat channel is prefixed with a hash mark, #.

clickstream – The sequence of hyperlinks clicked by someone when using the internet.

click through This is when someone clicks on a banner ad or other link, for example, and is moved from that page to the advertiser's web site.

client – This is the term given to any program that you use to access the internet. For example your web browser is a web client, your email program is an email client, your newsreader is a news client, and your chat software is a chat client.

community – The internet is often described as a net community. This refers to the fact that many people like the feeling of belonging to a group of like-minded individuals. Many big web sites have been developed along these lines, such as GeoCities at: www.geocities.com

compression – Computer files can be electronically compressed, so that they can be uploaded or downloaded more quickly across the internet, saving time and money. If an image file is compressed too much, there may be a loss of quality. To use them, you uncompress 'unzip' them.

configure – To set up, or adjust the settings of, a computer or software program.

content – The articles, messages, forums, images, text, hyperlinks and other features of a web site.

cookie – A cookie is a small text code that a web server writes to your hard drive in order to track your use of its web site.

cracker – Someone who breaks into computer systems with the intention of causing some kind of damage or system abuse.

crash – What happens when a computer program malfunctions. The operating system of your PC may perform incorrectly or come to a complete stop ('freeze'), forcing you to shut down and restart.

cross-posting – Posting an identical message in several different newsgroups or mailing lists at the same time.

cybercash – This is a trademark, but is also often used as a broad term to describe the use of small payments made over the internet using a new form of electronic account that is loaded up with cash. You can send this money to the companies offering such cash facilities by cheque, or by credit card. Some internet companies offering travel-related items can accept electronic cash of this kind.

cyberspace – Popular term for the intangible 'place' where you go to surf - the ethereal and borderless world of computers and telecommunications on the internet.

cypherpunk – From the cypherpunk mailing list charter: ' Cypherpunks assume privacy is a good thing and wish there were more of it. Cypherpunks acknowledge that those who want privacy must create it for themselves and not expect governments, corporations, or other large, faceless organisations to grant them privacy out of beneficence.'

cypherpunk remailer – Cypherpunk remailers strip headers from the messages and add new ones.

cybersquatting Using someone else's name or trademark as your domain name in the hope they will buy it from you.

cyberstalker – An individual who pursues someone using online methods such as email, chat rooms and newsgroups.

data – Pieces of information (singular: datum). Data can exist in many forms such as numbers in a spreadsheet, text in a document, or as binary numbers stored in a computer's memory.

database – A store of information in digital form. Many web sites make use of substantial databases to deliver maximum content at high speed to the web user.

dial up account – This allows you to connect your (local) computer to your internet service provider's (remote) computer.

digital – Based on the two binary digits, 1 and 0. The operation of all computers is based on this amazingly simple concept. All forms of information are capable of being digitised - numbers, words, and even sounds and images - and then transmitted over the internet.

digital signature – A unique and secure personal signature specially created for use over the internet. It is designed to fulfil a similar function to that of the traditional handwritten signature.

directory – On a PC, a folder containing your files.

DNS – Domain name server.

domain name – A name that identifies an IP address. It identifies to the computers on the rest of the internet where to access particular information. Each domain has a name. For someone@somewhere.co.uk, 'somewhere' is the domain name.

download – Downloading means copying a file from one computer on the internet to your own computer. You do this by clicking on a button that links you to the appropriate file. Downloading is an automatic process, except that you have to click ' yes' to accept the download and give it a file name. You can download any type of file - text, graphics, sound, spreadsheet, computer programs, and so on.

ebusiness The broad concept of doing business to business, and business to consumer sales, over the internet.

ecash – Short for electronic cash. See cybercash.

Echelon – The name of a massive governmental surveillance facility based in Yorkshire, UK. Operated clandestinely by the US, UK and certain other governments, it is said to be eavesdropping virtually the entire traffic of the internet, using electronic dictionaries to trawl through millions of emails and other transmissions.

ecommerce The various means and techniques of transacting business online.

email – Electronic mail, any message or file you send from your computer to another computer using your email client program (such as Netscape Messenger or Microsoft Outlook).

email address The unique address given to you by your ISP. It can be used by others using the internet to send email messages to you. An email address always has at 'at' sign in the middle, for example:

myname@myISP.com

email bomb – An attack by email whereby someone is sent hundreds or thousands of email messages in a very short period of time. Such an attack could prevent that person from receiving genuine email messages.

emoticons – Popular symbols used to express emotions in email, for example

Dial-Up
Networking

the well known smiley:

:-)

which means 'I'm smiling!' or ' Don't take this too seriously'. Emoticons are not normally appropriate for business communications.

encryption – The scrambling of information to make it unreadable without a key or password. Email and any other data can now be encrypted using PGP and other freely available programs. Modern encryption has become so amazingly powerful as to be to all intents and purposes uncrackable.

Excite – A popular internet directory and search engine used to find pages relating to specific keywords which you enter. See: www.excite.com

ezines – The term for magazines and newsletters published on the internet.

FAQs – Frequently asked questions. You will see ' FAQ' everywhere you go on the internet. If you are ever doubtful about anything check the FAQ page, if the site has one, and you should find the answers to your queries.

favorites – The rather coy term for **bookmarks** used by Internet Explorer, and by America Online. Maintaining a list of Favorites is designed to make returning to web sites easier, by saving their addresses.

file – A file is any body of data such as a word processed document, a spreadsheet, a database file, a graphics or video file, sound file, or computer program. On a PC, every file has a filename, and a filename extension showing what type of file it is.

filtering software – Software loaded onto a computer to prevent access by someone to unwelcome content on the internet, notably porn. The well-known ' parental controls' include CyberSitter, CyberPatrol, SurfWatch and NetNanny. They can be blunt instruments. For example, if they are programmed to reject all web pages containing the word ' virgin', you would not be able to access any web page hosted at Richard Branson's Virgin Net! Of course, there are also web sites that tell you step-by-step how to disable or bypass these filtering tools, notably: www.peacefire.org

finger – A tool for locating people on the internet. The most common use is to see if a person has an account at a particular internet site. It also means a chat command that returns information about the other chat user, including idle time (time since they last did anything).

firewall – A firewall is special security software designed to stop the flow of certain files into and out of a computer network, e.g. viruses or attacks by hackers. A firewall would be an important feature of any fully commercial web site.

flame – A more or less hostile or aggressive message posted in a newsgroup or to an individual newsgroup user.

folder – The name for a directory on a computer. It is a place in which files are stored.

form – A web page that allows or requires you to enter information into fields on the page and send the information to a web site, program or individual on the web. Forms are often used for registration or sending questions and comments to web sites.

forums – Places for discussion on the internet. They include Usenet newsgroups, mailing lists, and bulletin board services.

frames – A web design feature in which web pages are divided into several areas or panels, each containing separate information. A typical set of frames in a page includes an index frame (with navigation links), a banner frame (for a heading), and a body frame (for text matter).

freespace – An allocation of free web space by an internet service provider or other organisation, to its users or subscribers, typically between 5 and 20 megabytes.

freeware – Software programs made available without charge. Where a small charge is requested, the term is **shareware**.

Glossary of internet terms ....

front page – The first page of your web site that the visitor will see. FrontPage is also the name of a popular web authoring package from Microsoft.

FTP – File transfer protocol the method the internet uses to speed files back and forth between computers. Your browser will automatically select this method, for instance, when you want to download your bank statements to reconcile your accounts. In practice you don't need to worry about FTP unless you are thinking about creating and publishing your own web pages: then you would need some of the freely available FTP software. Despite the name, it's easy to use.

GIF – Graphic interchange format. It is a widely-used compressed file format used on web pages and elsewhere to display files that contain graphic images. See also **JPEG** and **MPEG**.

GUI – Short for graphic user interface. It describes the user-friendly screens found in Windows and other WIMP environments (Windows, icons, mice, pointers).

hacker – A person interested in computer programming, operating systems, the internet and computer security. The term can be used to describe a person who breaks into computer systems with the intention of pointing out the weaknesses in a system. In common usage, the term is often wrongly used to describe crackers.

header – That part of an email message or newsgroup posting which contains information about the sender and the route that the message took across the internet.

history list – A record of visited web pages. Your browser probably includes a history list. It is handy way of revisiting sites whose addresses you have forgotten to bookmark - just click on the item you want in the history list. You can normally delete all or part of the history list in your browser. Your ISP may well be analysing this information even if you delete it on your own computer (see **internet service providers**, above).

hit counter – A piece of software used by a web site to record the number of hits it has received.

hits – The number of times pieces of text, images, hyperlinks and other components of a web page have been viewed. A better measure of a site's popularity would be the number of page views, or the number of user sessions.

home page This refers to the index page of an individual or an organisation on the internet. It usually contains links to related pages of information, and to other relevant sites

host – A host is the computer where a particular file or domain is located, and from where people can retrieve it.

HotBot – A popular internet search engine used to find pages relating to any keywords you decide to enter.

HTML – Hyper text markup language, the universal computer language used to create pages on the world wide web. It is much like word processing, but uses special ' tags' for formatting the text and creating hyperlinks to other web pages.

HTTP – Hypertext transfer protocol, the protocol used by the world wide web. It is the language spoken between your browser and the web servers. It is the standard way that HTML documents are transferred from host computer to your local browser when you're surfing the internet. You'll see this acronym at the start of every web address, for example:

http://www.abcxyz.com

With modern browsers, it is no longer necessary to enter ' http://' at the start of the address.

hyperlink – See **link**.

hypertext – This is a link on an HTML page that, when clicked with a mouse, results in a further HTML page or graphic being loaded into view on your browser.

IANA The Internet Assigned Numbers Authority, the official body responsible for ensuring that the numerical coding of the internet works properly.

ICANN The committee that oversees the whole domain name system.

ICQ – A form of internet chat, derived from the phrase 'I seek you'. It enables users to be alerted whenever fellow users go online, so they can have instant chat communication. The proprietary software is owned by America Online.

impression An internet advertising term that means the showing of a single instance of an advert on a single computer screen.

Infoseek – One of the ten most popular internet search engines, now teamed up with Disney in the GO Network.

Intel – Manufacturer of the Pentium and Celeron microprocessors used in millions of personal computers.

internet – The broad term for the fast-expanding network of global computers that can access each other in seconds by phone and satellite links. If you are using a modem on your computer, you too are part of the internet. The general term 'internet' encompasses email, the world wide web, internet chat, Usenet newsgroups, mailing lists, bulletin boards, telnet, and video conferencing. It is rather like the way we speak of 'the printed word' when we mean books, magazines, newspapers, newsletters, catalogues, leaflets, tickets and posters. The 'internet' does not exist in one place any more than 'the printed word' does.

Internet2 – A new form of the internet being developed exclusively for educational and academic use.

internet account – The account set up by your internet service provider which gives you access to the world wide web, electronic mail facilities, newsgroups and other value added services.

internet directory – A special web site which consists of information about other sites. The information is classified by subject area and further subdivided into smaller categories. The biggest and most widely used is Yahoo! - www.yahoo.com – – See also **search engines**.

Internet Explorer – The world's most popular browser software, a product of Microsoft and leading the field against Netscape.

internet keywords – A commercial service that allows people to find your domain name without having to type in www or .com

Internet protocol number – The numerical code that is a web site's real domain name address, rather than its alphabetical name.

internet service providers – ISPs are commercial, educational or official organisations which offer people ('users') access to the internet. The well-known commercial ones include AOL, CompuServe, BT Internet, Freeserve, Demon and Virgin Net. Services typically include access to the world wide web, email and newsgroups, as well as others such as news, chat, and entertainment. Your internet service provider is able to know everything you do on the internet, involving challenging new issues of personal privacy and data protection.

intranet – Software that uses internet technology to allow communication between individuals, for example within a commercial organisation. It often operates on a LAN (local area network).

IP address – An 'internet protocol' address. All computers linked to the internet have one. The address is somewhat like a telephone number, and consists of four sets of numbers separated by dots. Your ISP probably allocates you a different temporary ('dynamic') IP address each time you log on.

IPv6 – The new internet coding system that will allow even more domain names.

IRC – Internet relay chat. Chat is an enormously popular part of the internet, and there are all kinds of chat rooms and chat software. The chat involves typing messages which are sent and read in real time. It was developed in 1988 by

Glossary of internet terms ....

Jarkko Oikarinen.

ISDN Integrated services digital network. This is a high-speed telephone network that can send computer data from the internet to your PC faster than a normal telephone line.

Java A programming language developed by Sun Microsystems to use the special properties of the internet to create graphics and multimedia applications on web sites.

JavaScript A simple programming language that can be put onto a web page to create interactive effects such as buttons that change appearance when you position the mouse over them.

JPEG – The acronym is short for Joint Photographic Experts Group. A JPEG is a specialised file format used to display graphic files on the internet. JPEG files can be smaller than similar GIF files and so have become ever more popular - even though their quality may not be as good as GIF format files. See also MPEG.

key shortcut Two keys pressed at the same time. Usually the Control key (Ctrl), Alt key, or Shift key combined with a letter or number. For example, to use Control-D, press Control, tap the D key once firmly, then take your finger off the Control key.

keywords – Words that sum up your web site for being indexed in search engines. For example for a cosmetic site the keywords might include beauty, lipstick, make-up, fashion, cosmetic and so on.

kick – To eject someone from a chat channel.

LAN – A local area network, a computer network usually located in one building or campus.

link – A hypertext phrase or image that calls up another web page when you click on it. Most web sites have lots of hyperlinks - links for short. These appear on the screen as buttons, images or bits of text (often underlined) that you can click on with your mouse to jump to another site on the world wide web.

Linux – A new widely and freely available operating system for personal computers, and a potentially serious challenger to Microsoft. It has developed a considerable following.

LINX – The London Internet Exchange, the facility which maintains UK internet traffic in the UK. It allows existing individual internet service providers to exchange traffic within the UK, and improve connectivity and service for their customers. LINX is one of the largest and fastest growing exchange points in Europe, and maintains connectivity between the UK and the rest of the world.

listserver – An automated email system whereby subscribers are able to receive and send email from other subscribers to the same mailing list. See: www.liszt.com

log on/log off – To access/leave a network. In the early days of computing this literally involved writing a record in a log book. You may be asked to ' log on' to certain sites and particular pages. This normally means entering your user ID in the form of a name and a password.

lurk – The term used to describe reading the messages in a newsgroup without actually posting messages yourself.

macros – ' Macro languages' are used to automate repetitive tasks in Word processors and other applications. They can carry viruses.

mail server – A remote computer that enables you to send and receive emails. Your internet access provider will usually act as your mail server, storing your incoming messages until you go online to retrieve them.

mailing list A forum where messages are distributed by email to the members of the forum. The two types of lists are discussion and announcement. Discussion lists allow exchange between list members. Announcement lists are one-way only and used to distribute information such as news or humour. A good place to find mailing lists is Liszt: www.liszt.com

marquee – A moving (scrolling) line of text on a web site, normally used for advertising purposes.

Media Player – Windows software on a personal computer that will play sounds and images including video clips and animations.

metasearch engine – A site that sends a keyword search to many different search engines and directories so you can use many search engines from one place.

meta tags The technical term for the keywords used in web page code to help search engine software rank the site.

Microsoft – A najor producer of software for personal computers, including the Windows operating systems, and the web browser Internet Explorer.

Mixmaster – An anonymous remailer that sends and receives email messages as packages of exactly the same size and often randomly varies the delay time between receiving and remailing to make interception harder.

modem – This is an internal or external piece of hardware plugged into your PC. It links into a standard phone socket, thereby giving you access to the internet. The word derives from MOdulator and DEModulator.

moderator – A person in charge of a mailing list, newsgroup or forum. The moderator prevents unwanted messages.

MPEG or **MPG** – A file format used for video clips available on the internet. See also JPEG.

MP3 – An immensely popular audio format that allows you to download and play music on your computer. It compresses music to create files that are small yet whose quality is almost as good as CD music. At the time of writing, MP4, even faster to download was being developed. See the consumer web site: www.mp3.com

navigate – To click on the hyperlinks on a web site in order to move to other web pages or internet sites.

net – A slang term for the internet. In the same way, the world wide web is often just called the web.

netiquette – Popular term for the unofficial rules and language people follow to keep electronic communication in an acceptably polite form.

Netmeeting – This Microsoft plug in allows a moving video picture to be contained within a web page. It is now integrated into Windows Media Player.

Netscape – After Microsoft's Internet Explorer, Netscape is the most popular browser software available for surfing the internet. It has suffered in the wake of Internet Explorer, in part because of the success of Microsoft in getting the latter pre-loaded on most new PCs. Netscape Communicator comes complete with email, newsgroups, address book and bookmarks, plus a web page composer. Netscape is now part of American Online.

newbie – Popular term for a new member of a newsgroup or mailing list.

newsgroup – A Usenet discussion group. Each newsgroup is a collection of messages, usually unedited and not checked by anyone (' unmoderated'). Anyone can post – messages to a newsgroup. It is rather like reading and sending public emails. The ever-growing newsgroups have been around for much longer than the world wide web, and are an endless source of information, gossip, news, entertainment, sex, scandal, politics, resources and ideas. The 80,000-plus newsgroups are collectively referred to as Usenet, and millions of people use it every day.

newsreader – A type of software that enables you to search, read, post and manage messages in a newsgroup. It will normally be supplied by your internet service provider when you first sign up, or preloaded on your new computer. The best known newsreaders are Microsoft Outlook, and Netscape Messenger.

news server – A remote computer (e.g. your internet service provider) that enables you to access newsgroups. If you cannot get some or any newsgroups from your existing news server, use your favourite search engine to search for ' open news servers' - there are lots available.

nick – Nickname, an alias you can give yourself and use to protect your personal privacy when entering a chat channel, rather than using your real name.

Nominet – The official body for registering domain names in the UK, for example web sites whose name ends in .co.uk.

Notepad – The most basic type of word processor that comes with a Windows PC. To find it, click Start, Programs, then Accessories. Its very simplicity makes it ideal for writing and saving HTML pages.

online – The time you spend linked via a modem to the internet. You can keep your phone bill down by reducing online time. The opposite term is offline.

open source software – A type of freely modifiable software, such as Linux. A definition and more information can be found at: www.opensource.org

OS – The operating system in a computer, for example MS DOS (Microsoft Disk Operating System), or Windows 95/98/2000.

packet – The term for any small piece of data sent or received over the internet on your behalf by your internet service provider. It contains your address and the recipient's address. One email message for example may be transmitted as several different packets of information, and reassembled at the other end to recreate the message. The contents of packets can be detected by sniffer software, as used for example by ISPs and government surveillance agencies.

parking – Placing a web domain into storage until it is wanted for public use at a later date.

password – A word or series of letters and numbers that enables a user to access a file, computer or program. A passphrase is a password made by using more than one word.

patch – A small piece of software used to patch up a hole or defect (' bug') in a software program.

PC – Personal computer, based on IBM technology. It is distinct from the Apple Macintosh which uses its own different operating system.

PDA – Personal data assistant a mobile phone, palm top or any other hand-held processor, typically used to access the internet.

PDF – Portable document format, a handy type of file produced using Adobe Acrobat software.

Pentium – The name of a very popular microprocessor chip in personal computers, manufactured by Intel. The first Pentium IIIs were supplied with unique personal identifiers, which ordinary people surfing the net were unwittingly sending out, enabling persons unknown to construct detailed user profiles. After protests, Pentium changed the technology so that this identifier could be disabled.

PGP – Pretty Good Privacy. A proprietary and free method of encoding a message before transmitting it over the internet. With PGP, a message is first compressed then encoded with the help of a pair of keys. Just like the valuables in a locked safe, your message is safe unless a person has access to the right keys. Many governments now want access to people's private keys. See: www.pgpi.com

ping – A ping test is used to check the connection speed between one computer and another.

plugin – A type of (usually free and downloadable) software required to add some form of functionality to web page viewing. A well-known example is Macromedia Shockwave, a plugin that enables you to view animations.

PoP – Point of presence. This refers to the dial-up phone numbers available from your ISP. If your ISP does not have a local point of presence (i.e. local access phone number), then don't sign up - your telephone bill will rocket because you will be charged national phone rates. All the major ISPs have local numbers covering the whole of the country.

portal site – Portal means gateway. It is a web site designed to be used as a base from which to explore the internet, or some particular part of it. Yahoo! is a good example of a portal (www.yahoo.com). A portal site includes the one that loads into your browser each time you connect to the internet. It could for example be the front page of your internet service provider.

post – The common term used for sending ('posting') messages ('articles') to a newsgroup. Posting messages is very like sending emails, except of course that they are public and everyone can read them. Also, newsgroup postings are archived, and can be read by anyone in the world years later. Because of this, many people feel more comfortable using an ' alias' (made-up name) when posting messages. See: www.deja.com

privacy – Unless you take steps to protect yourself, you have little personal privacy online. All your activity online is liable to be logged, analysed and possibly archived by internet organisations, government and surveillance services. You are also leaving a permanent trail of data on your computer. But then, if you have nothing to hide you have nothing to fear To explore privacy issues worldwide visit the authoritative Electronic Frontier Foundation web site: www.eff.org For the UK see: www.netfreedom.org

program – A series of coded instructions designed to automatically control a computer in carrying out a specific task. Programs are written in special languages including Java, JavaScript VBScript, and ActiveX.

protocol – On the internet, a protocol means a set of technical rules that has been agreed and is used between participating systems. For example, for viewing web pages your computer would use hypertext transfer protocol (http). For downloading and uploading files, it would use file transfer protocol (ftp).

proxy – An intermediate computer or server, used for reasons of security.

Quicktime – A popular free software program from Apple Computers. It is designed to play sounds and images including video clips and animations on both Apple Macs and personal computers.

radio button – A button that, when clicked, looks like this: ⊙

refresh, reload – The refresh or reload button on your browser toolbar tells the web page you are looking at to reload.

register – You may have to give your name, personal details and financial information to some sites before you can continue to use the pages. Site owners may want to produce a mailing list to offer you products and services. Registration is also used to discourage casual traffic. A high proportion of internet users enter fictional details to protect their privacy.

registered user – Someone who has filled out an online form and then been granted permission to access a restricted area of a web site. Access is usually obtained by logging on, typically by entering a password and user name.

remailer – A remailer is an internet service that preserves your privacy by acting as a go-between when you browse or send email messages. An anonymous remailer is simply a computer connected to the internet that can forward an email message to other people after stripping off the header of the messages. Once a message is routed through an anonymous remailer, the recipient of that message, or anyone intercepting it, can no longer identify its origin.

RFC – Request for comment. RFCs are the way that the internet developers propose changes and discuss standards and procedures. See: http://rs.internic.-net

RSA – One of the most popular methods of encryption, and used in Netscape browsers. See: www.rsa.com

router – A machine that directs all internet data (packets) from one internet location to another.

rules – The term for message filters in Outlook Express.

script – A script is a set of commands written into the HTML tags of a web page. Script languages such as JavaScript and VBScript work in a similar way to macros in a word processor. Scripts are hidden from view but are executed when you open a page or click a link containing script instructions.

scroll, scroll bar – To scroll means to move part of a page or document into view, or out of view, on the screen. Scrolling is done by using a scroll bar activated by the mouse pointer. Grey scroll bars automatically appear on the right and/ or lower edge of the screen if the page contents are too big to fit into view.

search engine – A search engine is a web site you can use for finding something on the internet. The information-gathering technology variously involves the use of ' bots' (search robots), spiders or crawlers. Popular search engines and internet directories have developed into big web sites and information centres in their own right. There are hundreds of them. Among the best known are AltaVista, Excite, Google, HotBot, – Infoseek , Lycos, Metasearch, Webcrawler and Yahoo!.

secure servers – The hardware and software provided so that people can use their credit cards and leave other details without the risk of others seeing them online. Your browser will flash up a reassuring notice when you are entering a secure site.

secure sockets layer (SSL) – A standard piece of technology which ensures secure financial transactions and data flow over the internet.

security certificate – Information that is used by the SSL protocol to establish a secure connection. Security certificates contain information about who it belongs to, who it was issued by, some form of unique identification, valid dates, and an encrypted fingerprint that can be used to verify the contents of the certificate.

server – Any computer on a network that provides access and serves information to other computers.

shareware – Software that you can try before you buy. Usually there is some kind of limitation such as an expiry date. To get the registered version, you must pay for the software, typically $20 to $40. A vast amount of shareware is now available online.

Shockwave – A popular piece of software produced by Macromedia, which enables you to view animations and other special effects on web sites. You can download this plugin for free, and in a few minutes, from Macromedia's web site. The effects can be fun, but they may slow down the speed at which the pages load into your browser window. See: www.macromedia.com

signature file – This is a little text file in which you can place your address details, for adding to email and newsgroup messages. Once you have created a signature file, it is automatically appended to your emails. You can of course delete or edit it at any time.

Slashdot – One of the leading technology news web sites. See: http://slashdot.org

smiley – A form of **emoticon**.

snail mail – The popular term for the standard postal service involving post-persons, vans, trains, planes, sacks and sorting offices.

sniffer – A program on a computer system (usually an ISP's system) designed to collect information. Sniffers are often used by hackers to harvest passwords and user names, and by surveillance agencies to target internet – activity.

spam –The popular term for electronic junk mail - unsolicited and unwelcome email messages sent across the internet. There are various forms of spam-busting software which you can now obtain to filter out unwanted email messages.

SSL – Secure socket layer, a key part of internet security technology.

subscribe – The term for accessing a newsgroup in order to read and post – messages in the newsgroup. There is no charge, and you can subscribe, unsubscribe and resubscribe at will with a click of your mouse. Unless you post a message, no-one in the newsgroup will know that you have subscribed or unsubscribed.

surfing – Slang term for browsing the internet, especially following trails of links on pages across the world wide web.

sysop – Systems operator, someone rather like a moderator for example of a chat room or bulletin board service.

talkers – Chat servers which give users the opportunity to talk to each other. You connect to them, take a 'nickname' and start chatting. Usually, they offer some other features besides just allowing users to talk to each other, including bulletin boards, a virtual world such as a city or building, which you move around in, an opportunity to store some information on yourself, and some games.

TCP/IP – Transmission control protocol/internet protocol, the essential communication rules of the internet.

telnet – Software that allows you to connect across the internet to a remote computer (e.g. a university department or library). You can then access that computer as if you were on a local terminal linked to that system.

template – A pre-designed page which you can adapt in various ways to suit your own needs. Templates are widely used, for example, in popular web authoring packages such as Microsoft Front Page Express.

theme – A term in web page design. A theme describes the general colours and graphics used within a web site. Many themes are available in the form of readymade templates.

thread – An ongoing topic in a Usenet newsgroup or mailing list discussion. The term refers to the original message on a particular topic, and all the replies and other messages which spin off from it. With newsreading software, you can easily 'view thread' and thus read the related messages in a convenient batch.

thumbnail – A small version of a graphic file which, when clicked on screen, displays a larger version.

top level domain – The last element of a web site's domain name, such as .com or .uk or .net

traceroute – A program that traces the route from your machine to a remote system. It is useful if you need to discover a person's ISP, for example in the case of a spammer.

traffic – The amount of data flowing across the internet, to a particular web site, newsgroup or chat room, or as emails.

trojan horse – A program that seems to perform a useful task but which in fact disguises a malevolent program designed to cause damage to a computer system.

UNIX This is a computer operating system that has been in use for many years, and still is used in many larger systems. Most ISPs use it.

uploading The act of copying files from your PC to a server or other PC on the internet, for example when you are publishing your own web pages. It describes the act of copying HTML pages onto the internet via FTP.

URL – Uniform resource locator the address of each internet page. For instance the URL of Internet Handbooks is: http://www.internet-handbooks.co.uk

Usenet – The collection of well over 80,000 active newsgroups that make up a substantial part of the internet.

virtual reality – The presentation of a lifelike scenario in electronic form. It can be used for gaming, business or educational purposes.

Glossary of internet terms ....

virtual server A portion of a PC that is used to host your own web domain (if you have one).

virus – A computer program maliciously designed to cause havoc to people's computer files. Viruses can typically be received when downloading program files from the internet, or from copying material from infected disks. Even Word files can be infected through macros. You can protect yourself from the vast majority of them by installing some inexpensive anti-virus software, such as produced by Norton, McAfee or Dr Solomon.

web authoring – Creating HTML pages to upload onto the internet. You will be a web author if you create your own home page for uploading onto the internet.

web – Short for the world wide web. See **WWW** below.

WAP – Wireless application protocol, new technology that enables mobile phones and other portal gadgets to access the internet.

web-based chat – A form of internet chat which just uses web pages, and does not require special software like IRC and ICQ. For web-based chat, the settings in your browser must be Java-enabled. Most modern browsers are Java-enabled by default.

web client – Another term for a web browser.

Webcrawler – A popular internet search engine used to find pages relating to specific keywords entered.

webmaster – Any person who manages a web site.

web page – Any single page of information you can view on the world wide web. A typical web page includes a unique URL (address), headings, text, images, and hyperlinks (usually in the form of graphic icons, or underlined text). One web page usually contains links to lots of other web pages, either within the same web site or elsewhere on the world wide web.

web rings – A network of interlinked web sites that share a common interest. See: www.webring.org

web site – A set of web pages, owned or managed by the same person or organisation, and which are interconnected by hyperlinks.

whois – A network service that allows you to consult a database containing information about someone. A whois query can, for example, help to find the identity of someone who is sending you unwanted email messages.

Windows – The ubiquitous operating system for personal computers developed by Bill Gates and the Microsoft Corporation. The Windows 3.1 version was followed by Windows 95 and 98. Windows 2000 is the latest.

wizard – A feature of many software programs that steps you through its main stages, for example with the use of readymade templates or options.

WWW – The world wide web. Since it began in 1994 this has become the most popular part of the internet. The web is now made up of more than a billion web pages of every imaginable description, typically linking to other pages.

WYSIWYG – 'What you see is what you get.' If you see it on the screen, then it should look just the same when you print it out.

Yahoo! – Probably the world's most popular internet directory and search engine, valued on Wall Street at billions of dollars: www.yahoo.com

zip/unzip – Many files that you download from the internet will be in compressed format, especially if they are large files. This is to make them quicker to download. Unzipping these compressed files means restoring them to their original size. Zip files usually have the extension '.zip' and are easily handled by using WinZip or a similar proprietary software package. See: www.winzip.-com

Index

Index . . . .

Creating a Home Page on the Internet
An illustrated step-by-step guide for beginners
Richard Cochrane BA (Hons) PhD

Have you just started to use the internet? If so you will soon be wondering how you can produce and publish web pages of your own, as millions of other individuals have done all over the world. It's easy! Discover how to design a simple but effective home page; see how to add your own artwork and photographs; learn how to add those magic hypertext links that enable you to click effortlessly from one web page to another. Finally, explore how you can actually publish your own home pages in cyberspace, where potentially anyone in the world can pay you a 'visit' and contact you by email.
1 84025 309 6

Education & Training on the Internet
An essential resource for students, teachers, and education providers
Laurel Alexander MIPD MICG

Confused by search engines? Fed up with floods of irrelevant information? This is a much-needed new guide to today's exploding new world of education and training online. It includes reviews of top web sites of every imaginable kind – for education and training providers, schools, colleges, universities, training centres, professional organisations, resource suppliers, individuals, business organisations and academic institutions. Whether you are planning to study online, or are planning the delivery of online education and training, you will find this a key resource. Laurel Alexander MIPD MICG is a qualified trainer, assessor and guidance specialist.
1 84025 346 0

Finding a Job on the Internet (2nd edition)
Amazing new possibilities for jobseekers everywhere
Brendan Murphy BSc (Hons) MBA MBSC

Thinking of looking for a new job, or even a change of career? The internet is a great place to start your job search. Now in a new edition, this new guide explains how to find and use internet web sites and newsgroups to give you what you need. School, college and university leavers will find it invaluable for identifying suitable employers and getting expert help with CVs and job applications. The book will also be useful for career advisers and employers thinking of using the internet for recruitment purposes. Brendan Murphy BSc MBA MBSC teaches HNC in Computing, and lectures for the Open University.
1 84025 365 7

Homes & Property on the Internet
A guide to 1000s of top web sites for buyers, sellers, owners, tenants, sharers, holiday makers & property professionals
Philip Harrison

Here is a guide to today's whole new world of homes and property services online. It reviews web sites of every imaginable kind for estate agents, house builders, solicitors, town planners, architects and surveyors, banks and building societies, home shares, villa owners and renters, and property-related associations, pressure groups, newspapers and magazines. Whether you are planning to move house, or rent a holiday home, or locate property services in the UK or wider afield, this is the book for you – comprehensive and well-indexed to help you find what you want.
1 84025 335 5

Other Internet Handbooks . . . .

Law & Lawyers on the Internet
An essential guide and resource for legal practitioners
Stephen Hardy & Michael Base

Following the Woolf Reforms, efficient research and communication will be the key to future legal life. This handbook will meet the needs of solicitors, barristers, law students, public officials, community groups and consumers who are seeking guidance on how to access and use the major legal web sites and information systems available to them on the internet. It includes expert site reviews on law associations, law firms, case law and court reporting, European legal institutions, government, legal education and training, publishers, the courts and branches of the law. Don't leave for court without it! Stephen Hardy JP LLB PhD teaches law at Manchester University.
1 84025 345 2

The Internet for Students
Making the most of the new medium for study and fun
David Holland ACIB

Are you a student needing help with the internet to pursue your studies? Not sure where to start? – then this Internet Handbook is the one for you. It's up to date, full of useful ideas of places to visit on the internet, written in a clear and readable style, with plenty of illustrations and the minimum of jargon. It is the ideal introduction for all students who want to add interest to their studies, and make their finished work stand out, impressing lecturers and future employers alike. The internet is going to bring about enormous changes in modern life. As a student, make sure you are up to speed.
1 84025 306 1 – Reprinted

Using Email on the Internet
A step-by-step guide to sending and receiving messages and files
Kye Valongo

Email is one of the oldest parts of the internet. Most newcomers approach it with a bit of trepidation. But don't worry – it is quite straightforward and easy. Emailing is fast, cheap and convenient, and you'll soon wonder how you ever managed without it. Use this book to find out how to get started, how to successfully send and receive your first messages, how to send and receive attached files, how to manage your email folders, address book, user profiles, personal privacy, and lots more valuable skills. Kye Valongo is a qualified teacher, computer analyst, internet journalist and former Education Officer for IBM.
1 84025 300 2

Where to Find It on the Internet (2nd edition)
Your complete guide to search engines, portals, databases, yellow pages & other internet reference tools
Kye Valongo

Here is a valuable basic reference guide to hundreds of carefully selected web sites for everyone wanting to track down information on the internet. Don't waste time with fruitless searches – get to the sites you want, fast. This book provides a complete selection of the best search engines, online databases, directories, libraries, people finders, yellow pages, portals, and other powerful research tools. A recent selection of *The Good Book Guide*, and now in a new edition, this book will be an essential companion for all internet users, whether at home, in education, or in the workplace. Kye Valongo is a qualified teacher, computer analyst, internet journalist and former Education Officer for IBM.
1 84025 369 X